D0480193

CAMBRIDGE ECONOMIC HANDBOOKS.—VIII.
GENERAL EDITOR: J. M. KEYNES, M.A. C.B.

INTERNATIONAL ECONOMICS

INTERNATIONAL ECONOMICS

BY

R. F. HARROD

M.A.

STUDENT OF CHRIST CHURCH, OXFORD

WITH AN INTRODUCTION BY

J. M. KEYNES

M.A., C.B.

FELLOW OF KING'S COLLEGE, CAMBRIDGE

HARCOURT, BRACE AND COMPANY

NEW YORK

PRINTED IN THE UNITED STATES OF AMERICA
BY THE POLYGRAPHIC COMPANY OF AMERICA, N.Y.

INTRODUCTION TO THE SERIES

THE Theory of Economics does not furnish a body of settled conclusions immediately applicable to policy. It is a method rather than a doctrine, an apparatus of the mind, a technique of thinking, which helps its possessor to draw correct conclusions. It is not difficult in the sense in which mathematical and scientific techniques are difficult; but the fact that its modes of expression are much less precise than these, renders decidedly difficult the task of conveying it correctly to the minds of learners.

Before Adam Smith this apparatus of thought scarcely existed. Between his time and this it has been steadily enlarged and improved. Nor is there any branch of knowledge in the formation of which Englishmen can claim a more predominant part. This Series, however, is not directed towards making original contributions to economic science. Its object is to expound its elements in a lucid, accurate, and illuminating way, so that the number of those who can begin to think for themselves may be increased. It is intended to convey to the ordinary reader and to the uninitiated student some conception of the general principles of thought which economists now apply to economic problems. The writers have been more anxious to avoid obscure forms of expression than difficult ideas. Most of the omissions of matter often treated in textbooks are intentional; for as a subject develops, it is important, especially in books meant to be introductory, to discard the marks of the chrysalid stage before thought had wings.

Even on matters of principle there is not yet a complete unanimity of opinion amongst professional students of the subject. Immediately after the war daily economic events were of such a slashing character as to divert attention from theoretical complexities. But to-day, economic science has recovered its wind. Traditional treatments and traditional solutions are being questioned, improved, and revised. In the end this activity of research should clear up controversy. But for the moment controversy and doubt are increased. The writers of this series must apologise to the general reader and to the beginner if many parts of their subject have not yet reached to a degree of certainty and lucidity which would make them easy and straightforward reading.

J. M. KEYNES

CONTENTS

CHAPTER I

INTRODUCTORY

PAGE

§ 1. THE SCOPE OF THIS VOLUME 1

§ 2. INTERNATIONAL ECONOMICS AS A BRANCH OF
GENERAL ECONOMICS 4

§ 3. DISTINGUISHING FEATURES OF INTERNATIONAL
TRANSACTIONS 6

CHAPTER II

THE GAIN FROM FOREIGN TRADE

§ 1 IMPORTANCE OF THIS SUBJECT 10

§ 2 THE INTERNATIONAL DIVISION OF LABOUR . . 11

§ 3 THE LAW OF COMPARATIVE COSTS . . . 14

§ 4. A CALCULATION OF THE GAIN FROM FOREIGN
TRADE 20

§ 5. GAIN THROUGH DIFFERENCE OF COST RATIOS . 27

§ 6. ANOTHER EXAMPLE OF THE IMPORTANCE OF BEING
UNIMPORTANT 29

§ 7. THE GAIN FROM TRADE, AND COST GRADIENTS . 31

§ 8. THE GAIN FROM TRADE, AND DEMAND . . 35

§ 9. FOREIGN TRADE UNDER CONSTANT OR DECREASING
COSTS 37

§ 10 A MULTIPLICITY OF COMMODITIES INTRODUCED . 39

§ 11. CONCLUSIONS 40

CHAPTER III
POTENTIAL AND ACTUAL GAIN

PAGE

§ 1. TWO PROBLEMS 42

§ 2. THREE CONDITIONS NECESSARY FOR MAXIMIZING GAIN BY TRADE 43

§ 3. FULFILMENT OF CONDITIONS ABROAD NOT ESSENTIAL 47

§ 4. FAILURE OF CONDITIONS: (a) WHEN INDUSTRIES ARE GROWING OR DECLINING 49

§ 5. FAILURE OF CONDITIONS: (b) MONOPOLY . . 54

§ 6. SUMMARY 58

CHAPTER IV
COMPARATIVE PRICE LEVELS

§ 1. A CLASSIFICATION OF GOODS 59

§ 2. THE PRICE LEVEL OF INTERNATIONAL GOODS . 62

§ 3. THE PRICE LEVEL OF QUASI-INTERNATIONAL GOODS 65

§ 4. THE PRICE LEVELS OF DOMESTIC GOODS . . 67

§ 5. THE PRICE LEVELS OF FACTORS OF PRODUCTION . 71

§ 6. SUMMARY. 80

CHAPTER V
FOREIGN EXCHANGE

§ 1. THE BALANCE OF PAYMENTS (INTRODUCTORY) . 81

§ 2. THE GOLD STANDARD AND GOLD POINTS . . 85

§ 3. BILLS OF EXCHANGE 90

§ 4. FORWARD FOREIGN EXCHANGE . . . 93

§ 5. THE MONETARY SYSTEM 96

§ 6. THE CENTRAL BANK AND THE BALANCE OF PAYMENTS 99

§ 7. FOREIGN EXCHANGE IN THE ABSENCE OF A GOLD STANDARD 102

CHAPTER VI

THE BALANCE OF TRADE

PAGE
§ 1. THE EQUILIBRIUM IN SIMPLIFIED CONDITIONS . 104

§ 2. TRANSITION IN SIMPLIFIED CONDITIONS . . 115

§ 3. THE BALANCE OF PAYMENTS ON CURRENT ACCOUNT 118

§ 4. INTERNATIONAL CAPITAL MOVEMENTS . . 121

§ 5. THE BALANCE OF PAYMENTS AND DEFLATION . . 130

CHAPTER VII

WHEN THE GOLD STANDARD IS ABANDONED

§ 1. THE NEW FREEDOM 137

§ 2. STABILIZING THE VALUE OF MONEY. THE OBJECTIVE 140

§ 3. STABILIZING THE VALUE OF MONEY. THE MEANS . 151

CHAPTER VIII

WORLD MONETARY REFORM

§ 1. THE TRADE CYCLE 159

§ 2. THE MAINTENANCE OF MONETARY DEMAND . 162

§ 3. ALTERNATIVE PROJECTS 164

§ 4. PLAN FOR A COMMON STABLE WORLD MONEY . 166

§ 5. PLAN FOR A STABLE WORLD MONEY WITH NATIONAL
VARIATIONS 172

§ 6. GIVING EFFECT TO THE PLAN 177

CHAPTER IX
TARIFFS

PAGE

§ 1. ORIGINS 182

§ 2. TWO SPECIAL ARGUMENTS. (i) SELF-SUFFICIENCY.
(ii) BARGAINING 184

§ 3. TARIFFS AND THE BEST DISTRIBUTION OF PRODUCTIVE
RESOURCES 187

§ 4. TARIFFS AND THE FULL UTILIZATION OF PRODUCTIVE
RESOURCES 194

§ 5. SUMMARY OF CONCLUSIONS 201

APPENDIX 203

INDEX 209

INTERNATIONAL ECONOMICS

CHAPTER I

INTRODUCTORY

§ 1. *The Scope of this Volume.* It is proper at the outset to give some idea of the scope of this volume. The title does not sufficiently define it, for international economics is a large and complex subject; it might be surveyed from a historical or a geographical point of view; a brief description of the principal constituent items of international trade might be attempted; above all the reader might hope to find an analysis of the causes and phases of the present crisis, with a view to forming opinions about the probable course of events and the appropriate remedies for the situation. The purpose of this book is more precise and definite. As a preliminary to understanding aright the inner nature of particular events or to forming an intelligent opinion on matters of current controversy, it is necessary first to be apprised of certain simple and fundamental truths about international economic relations in general. It is to expound and elucidate these that an attempt is made here. The reader will find a treatment of what may be called the simple arithmetic of international economics. Far too much is commonly said and written in ignorance of or with complete disregard of this simple arithmetic.

The reader may console himself that the body of doctrine which he is asked to master is not a large one, nor is the intellectual effort required for the purpose great. It may be compared with that needed for the understanding of three or four theorems in elementary geometry. Yet that much effort is indispensable. The path is short but slippery. The subject is one in which fallacy and specious argumentation abound. Only by a thorough grasp of a few central propositions and of the means by which they are reached can immunity from the insidious attacks of quacks and propagandists be achieved. In pursuing a more developed branch of science, the student would not expect to be completely exempt from intellectual effort. Yet, really, the fact that the achievements of economics are exiguous and the tools used simple makes it necessary to concentrate all the more closely on what there is. Their complex technique of proof provides the conclusions of the more highly elaborated sciences with a defence against the inroads of charlatans. In economics fools are only too ready to rush in.

There has been much discussion as to whether economics should confine itself to the tracing of cause and effect or extend out into the practical sphere of advice and recommendation. Critics hold that, in making recommendations, economists are impinging on the region of ethics or politics. Controversy about method should, however, be settled, not on abstract grounds, but by reference to the achievements of the subject. Study of the most notable economic work reveals that it has in fact contained a large element of the practical recommendation. The objection to this rests on a misunderstanding. The phenomena studied by the economist are largely connected with human purposes, which in their interaction have given rise to a system of some complexity. When a change occurs in part of the system, it may be interesting to know, and appropriate for economists to study, what consequential changes are likely to occur in other parts of the system. It is also interesting to test the system by the criterion of how far the purposes which give rise to it find their fulfilment through it.

To test the system in this way is not to criticise the purposes themselves, which would, indeed, be an ethical matter. In studying the system, an approach may be made either by analysing the interaction of changes in its parts or by testing it with reference to its efficacy. The two approaches sometimes lead into the same terrain of analysis. It may be convenient now to adopt one, now another. Testing the system leads naturally on to making recommendations. Indeed the recommendations can often hardly be distinguished from a precise statement of how the system fails when the test is applied to it. In what follows the test method of approach is rather prominent. It is used in the analysis of the course of international trade and of the monetary system. The question is asked, what are the conditions in which trade takes such a course, that the purposes for which trade is admittedly undertaken are most fully realised ? Again, what is the kind of monetary system which best fulfils the purposes for which the use of money is admittedly devised ? No *a priori* justification for the procedure will be given ; it has in fact yielded the best results in this particular field. The recommendations which rise naturally out of such an examination contain no ethical element or political bias.

This book does not profess to break new ground in fundamental matters. But complete freedom is used in the mode in which established doctrines are set out, and it is possible that some of the secondary propositions are novel. The treatment of the direction and scope of foreign trade is based on the doctrines of the classical writers. These have been subjected to much criticism in the past, mostly of a pettifogging or terminological kind ; the main classical position in this sphere seems inexpugnable. The old economists were more concerned with the direction of trade than its volume. The connection between the volume of trade and the monetary system has only been worked out by more recent writers. In the later chapters, where this is dealt with, it is concluded that money should have stability of value. This appears to be the orthodoxy of the subject, if we trace the development of it in the best writers since Jevons. In the popular press other schools of thought, the deflationists, the so-called " sound currency " men, those who favour an " automatic " gold standard or a gold standard " worked according to the rules of the game " (are these the same ?), seem to have gained the reputation of orthodoxy. Their views find no favour in the following pages.

§ 2. *International Economics as a Branch of General Economics.* International economics is concerned with all economic transactions involving passage across a national frontier. Examples are emigration, the loan of capital by the nationals of one country to those of another, the purchase of goods by the nationals of one country from those of another. A set of infinitely vigilant frontier officials might be able, by examining all persons, cargoes and mail-bags entering or leaving Great Britain, to draw up an inventory of all the international economic transactions in which she was involved. It may at once occur to the reader that the findings of this company of officials might not be very different from those of another set whom we may imagine to have formed a cordon round the county of Warwick. They, too, would have their passengers, goods and mail-bags to examine, and they, too, would find migration, loans, the sale and purchase of goods, etc., in progress across the boundary. The Warwickshire inventory of transactions with the outer world would be quite similar to the British inventory. Nor need we stop at the Warwickshire example. A circular cordon might be described, having Rugby for its centre and ten miles for its radius, and a similar result could be achieved.

Clearly if international economics is to be justified as a proper subject of study, it is necessary to show that the transactions entered on the British inventory have attributes which make them differ substantially from transactions recorded in any of the similar inventories which might be drawn up on boundaries *not* coincident with national frontiers. In what ways do the economic transactions between people living under different national governments differ from those between people living under the same national governments, but in different localities?

It is important not to exaggerate the differences. For instance, there is one notable respect in which the international and, may we call them, inter-county transactions do not differ, namely, that the inward payments to which all give rise must roughly balance the outward payments,

the difference, if any, being covered by an actual remission
of money. Theories regarding the mechanism by which
the national balance of foreign payments is maintained
may be tested by applying them to any arbitrarily defined
area. If they implicitly assume the presence in every such
area of a mechanism which does not in fact exist, they
are properly suspect.

Moreover, it is also important to recognise the close
interconnexion between international and internal transactions. It would lead to disastrous errors to treat the
two in watertight compartments. The state of the
external world may affect not only the volume of our
imports and exports, but also such apparently domestic
matters as the yield of income-tax and the rate at which
new houses are constructed. Special attention will be
given to this interconnexion.

§ 3. *Distinguishing Features of International Transactions.*
What, then, are the distinguishing attributes of the
inventory of international transactions ?

(i). First and foremost, attention should be paid to the
migration figures, the movement of persons across the
boundaries. Temporary visits need not be considered
here. A number of persons born and bred in Warwickshire leave it to settle and earn their livelihood in other
parts of the kingdom, and vice versa. Similarly, each
year a number of persons emigrate from the kingdom to
seek their fortunes in other countries. But the volume of
inter-county movement, considered in proportion to the
size of the area affected, is much greater than that of the
international movement. Labour is more mobile between
the different parts of a national unit than between different
national units.

The reasons for this are sufficiently obvious. Barriers connected with language, national habits and sentiment, and, in recent times, stringent legal restrictions, obstruct the free flow of labour between different countries. The consequences are important. Within the national unit there is a tendency towards equality throughout the country in rewards to work, requiring given intensity and skill. Good opportunity for earning high rewards in one locality attracts movement to it from other parts of the country, and this movement sets up the tendency towards equalisation. But great differences in the rates of reward may subsist in different countries; the general level of real wages is roughly twice as high in New York as in London, roughly twice as high in London as in Rome. Such differences could not continue long in one country. What is true of the movement of labour applies, though in less degree, to the movement of capital and enterprise.

It follows that internal trade consists largely of the interchange of goods between producers who enjoy similar standards of life. International trade often consists of the interchange of goods between producers enjoying widely different standards. It is clear that the principles which determine the course and nature of these two kinds of interchange must be in some respects different.

This is the most important circumstance which makes a special study of international trade necessary. Analysis of internal trade assumes that there is a tendency towards an equal standard of living among those doing the same kind of work. The assumption may not accord with the facts precisely, but it is a workable approximation. In the case of international trade it has to be dropped entirely.

B

Similar standards may prevail in different countries, but there is no *a priori* probability that they will. The analysis of the advantages which accrue from international trade is independent of whether they do or not. The frequent claim that the import of goods made with cheap foreign labour should be checked thus implies ignorance of the first principles of the subject ; for it assumes that inequality of wages in two competing countries is abnormal, whereas in fact it is on the probable presence of that feature that the special study of international as distinct from internal trade is founded.

(ii) Special facilities for production may differ from place to place in one country and be similar in different countries, crossing political frontiers freely. But there are certain facilities and disabilities which are co-terminous with national frontiers, namely those connected with the activities of government. The citizens of one country are subject to the same system of national and local taxation, to the same regulations for health, sanitation, factory organisation, education, and social insurance, the same policy with regard to transport and public utilities, the same laws regarding industrial combination and trade unions, the same commercial code. Here is another basis for the distinction between internal and international trade. Even if capital and labour flowed freely between countries, so that wages, interest charges, profits, etc. were the same everywhere, the general level of real costs might be lower in one country than another, by reason of the superior advantages provided by the system of government. It would still be possible to distinguish between internal trade as interchange between producers provided by the government with similar amenities for production, and international trade as interchange between producers provided by the government with dissimilar amenities.

(iii) International transactions involving the payment of money are usually mediated by a foreign exchange transaction. Unless a common monetary standard is maintained, fluctuations in the rates at which national monies may be exchanged against each other clearly give a distinguishing mark to those transactions which are directly affected by the exchange rates.

Even if a common standard is in operation and foreign exchange fluctuations are confined within narrow limits, the fact that each national currency is controlled by its own government and central bank has special significance for international economics. The maintenance of the monetary standard involves the enforcement of a specific policy by the central bank ; an identical policy is not always required in all countries at the same time. This policy has repercussions on the whole economic life of the community to whose needs the central bank is administering. National areas are usually co-terminous with those controlled by a single central banking system. Thus, from one point of view, international transactions may be thought of as the class of all economic transactions between persons living in the spheres of influence of different central banks.

CHAPTER II

THE GAIN FROM FOREIGN TRADE

§ 1. *Importance of this Subject.* The question which I propose to put first is, what are the advantages to be derived from foreign trade ? It is convenient to do this, partly because the topic is one on which the most profound misconceptions prevail, partly because it is in its broad outline the simplest and most securely founded part of the subject of foreign trade, and also because it is well to bear the answer to this question in mind in considering and criticising the mechanism by which foreign trade is actually carried out and all or some of its potential advantages reaped.

Much popular writing on the subject of foreign trade shows considerable knowledge about the mechanism of foreign payments, the foreign exchanges, the balance of trade and circumstances likely to affect it, but no understanding whatever of what it is all for. Without a firm grasp of the origin and nature of the advantages that accrue from foreign trade, it is not possible to say much that is sensible about it. The reader is therefore asked at the outset to follow a discussion of the precise circumstances which determine the scope and degree of gain which foreign trade can be made to yield.

§ 2. *The International Division of Labour*. As exchange in general is necessitated by the division of labour, so foreign trade appears when the division of labour is pushed beyond national frontiers. It is the necessary consequence of an international division of labour. Two aspects of the division of labour may be mentioned. One is the splitting up of a productive process into parts, so as to simplify and thus render more effective the work which each labourer has to perform. The other is the adaptation of the productive system so as to give the greatest possible scope to those who have special talents or facilities for doing certain kinds of work.

It might be thought that the millions of workers which most nations can claim would suffice for the bare splitting up of the whole productive complex into conveniently simple parts. Adam Smith referred to the eighteen processes involved in pin-making ; this must be multiplied by an appropriate number to accord with modern conditions ; but, even if we multiplied the product by the number representing all the variety of different commodities which a community needs, we should be surprised if we found more productive processes in all than the number of workers in the whole community. This, however, would not be a fair procedure. Our demand for all commodities is not equal ; if the working population were divided in proportions corresponding to our demand for various products, it is possible that the number earmarked for making some product the demand for which is a minute proportion of the whole would not be sufficient to give the most economical division of labour in the making of that product. If a nation is to be self-sufficing, a large proportion of its workers must be engaged in making the main staple commodities, and the surplus left over for each of the various specialities might be inadequate, and so some international division of labour would be desirable.

By hypothesis, however, this cannot be the cause of international division of labour on a big scale. And so it is necessary to look to the other aspect of the division, namely the convenience of setting those with special facilities to do the tasks for which they are most fitted. Let each nation produce that which it can produce most cheaply.

Whence arise these special facilities ?

(i) Special facilities are provided by natural resources. Mines must be worked where they are found. This implies foreign trade, since the nations in whose territory the mines are situated must receive goods of some sort in exchange for the ores which they export. Many products, coffee, tea, rubber, etc., require a special climate for their cultivation.

Lands differ in natural fertility ; it is desirable that more fertile land should be worked more intensively. This by itself might not give rise to foreign trade, for the world's population might be distributed in proportion to the fertility of land, so as to provide a dense population for the rich soils to support and a thinner layer for poorer soils. It is not, however, permissible to suppose that the population of the world is in fact so distributed.

(ii) If mother earth yielded all things in equal abundance in all her parts, the uneven distribution of population would itself make foreign trade desirable. Certain productive processes, those of the extractive industries, must needs be conducted in close collaboration with the natural resources. Others, those concerned with the working up of raw materials into finished goods, can be conducted apart. Countries with a population dense in proportion to the capacity of the soil would naturally employ their surplus on the processes which do not have to be undertaken in close conjunction with the soil, and exchange manufactured goods for the raw products of more sparsely peopled regions.

(iii) Human capacity differs as well as that of the earth. The difference may be due to innate racial qualities of manual dexterity, scientific ability, vigour and enterprise, or to the political and social structure, itself the result of racial capacity for social organization or of the whole chain of historical accidents. Processes in which scientific skill or the capacity for conducting great collaborative enterprise—production on a large scale—counts for more in increasing efficiency should naturally be undertaken by the peoples more highly endowed with these qualities.

(iv) There is the legacy of the past. A nation may be bequeathed with a great structure of equipment, of factories and railways, or with a structure of organization, special knowledge and useful habit, constituting present aids to certain forms of production. The growth of this structure may have been due to good fortune or a natural superiority in the past, now vanished. But the legacy has not vanished. The inherited structure may give special facilities, which are as decisive a factor in determining its proper sphere of specialization as the presence of mines or oil-fields. If the peculiar advantages which aided the growth of this structure cease to exist, after a very long time the structure itself will disappear, just as a coal mine is finally worked out, and the nation will ultimately take its place among other nations bereft of this distinguishing feature.

If the greatest possible advantages of foreign trade are to be secured for all, each nation should devote itself to what it can do most cheaply. The expression " what it can do most cheaply " needs careful definition.

§ 3. *The Law of Comparative Costs.* Writers on foreign trade have usually found it convenient to develop this definition by considering in the first instance two nations producing two commodities. An alternative method is to consider the position of one country, say, England, in respect of two commodities *vis-à-vis* the rest of the world. The principle to be defined then becomes—England should produce for herself and for export what she can produce more cheaply, and import from abroad what can be produced more cheaply there.

The term, " abroad," is, of course, an abstraction. The outer world is not a homogeneous place but consists of a large number of particular countries, each with its own conditions. For the purpose of considering the gain from trade to England, it is convenient to suppose that the other countries have already entered into those trading relations which they think fit and have established some sort of equilibrium with each other, so that, for the purpose of isolating the phenomenon to be studied, we can compare the state of affairs when the rest of the world has all its complex relations but no trade with England, with that when the rest of the world has all its complex relations and its trade with England also.

It must be emphasized that this is an attempt to state what *should* happen, if full advantage is to be taken of the potentialities of the international division of labour. Whether that is what *does* happen, if trade is allowed to follow "its natural course," will be considered subsequently. Moreover, it may be held that it is not always desirable to take full advantage of the potentialities of the international division of labour, that it may be better to sacrifice increments of wealth in the interests of self-sufficiency. Such a consideration is beyond the immediate matter in hand.

Since this is an attempt to define comparative cheapness of production, it is necessary to have a unit for measuring cost of production. The same unit need not, and indeed cannot, be used for measuring cost at home and abroad. Cost may be measured in terms of trouble or effort or in terms of the reward that is paid for effort ; this reward may again be measured as so many baskets full of consumable goods, or as so much money. Happily for the present purpose it does not matter which method be adopted. All methods must presuppose that different kinds of cost, e.g. labour skilled and unskilled, waiting, the use of land or mines, can be measured against each other in the same country. Commodity A may take more land per unit of labour expended on it than commodity B. To compare the cost of producing A with that of producing B, we must be able to equate land to labour as elements in cost, to say that, for instance, 1 labourer per annum $=$ 100 acres per annum, or, $=$ 150 acres per annum. If the relative values of the various factors of production are determined, it is then possible to compare the cost of producing commodities A, B, C, etc., in the same country unequivocally.

The relative values of the factors may be different in different countries. Since the same unit will not be used for measuring the cost of producing commodities at home and abroad, this circumstance will not affect the argument.

To compare costs of production, units of the commodities must also be defined. Commodities are usually measured in tons, yards, etc., but for this purpose it is most convenient to take, as a unit of the commodity B, that amount of B which has in the first instance the same cost of production as a unit of the commodity A in England. Let us suppose that they each cost x units to produce. It is well to leave it undecided whether this means £x, x labour days, or x baskets full of commodities, etc.

Let the cost of producing a unit of A abroad be y units. The nature of the unit of cost is again left undefined. The following table represents the definitions given so far :

TABLE I

	Cost of production in England.	Cost of production Abroad.
Unit of commodity A .	x	y
Unit of commodity B .	x	–

The unit of B was defined as that amount of B which has the same cost of production in England as that of the chosen unit of A in England. Hence if the cost of producing a unit of A in England is x, that of producing a unit of B is also x. We have next to consider the cost of producing precisely these units of A and B abroad. We have supposed the cost of producing this unit of A to be y. So far nothing has been assumed about comparative cheapness at home or abroad. This will be determined by the fourth term which has to be inserted to make the table complete.

The fourth term may be equal to, greater than or less than y. If the cost of producing the unit of B abroad is y—

TABLE II

	Cost of production in England.	Cost of production Abroad.
Unit of commodity A	x	y
Unit of commodity B	x	y

no saving of cost can be gained by England taking on the production of either A or B for foreign consumption. It should be noted that this result has been arrived at without any assumption with regard to the relation of the cost of producing A in England to that of producing A abroad. It has not been asserted that y is equal to, less than, or greater than x; moreover, such an assertion would have been meaningless, for it is not known whether any common unit for measuring costs in the two countries can be found. If the relative values of labour, capital and land happen to be different in the two countries, no common unit is possible.

Suppose now that the " fourth term " is greater than y and equal to, say, $2y$:

TABLE III

	Cost of production in England.	Cost of production Abroad.
Unit of commodity A	x	y
Unit of commodity B	x	$2y$

Productive resources can be applied with equal efficacy to the production of units A or B in England ; but productive resources abroad are only half as efficacious in the production of these units of B as they are in that of these units of A. It follows from this that there will be a net increase in production if England takes over the production of B for foreign consumption and imports A in exchange. By transferring productive effort from B to A the foreigner produces twice as many units of A as he was producing of B; by transferring productive effort from A to B, England produces no less units of B than she formerly produced of A. How the benefits arising from the interchange will be distributed between England and the foreigner is discussed later.

But first the reader is asked to reconsider the tables, lest any misconception remain in his mind. Table III suggests, by reason of the notation adopted, that the Englishman is better placed than the foreigner, because on the whole he seems able to produce more cheaply. Nothing of the sort has been assumed. The units measured by x and y respectively are different units. y might equally well have been defined as the cost of producing a unit of B abroad. In that case the facts would be represented as follows :

TABLE IV

	Cost of production in England.	Cost of production Abroad.
Unit of commodity A	x	$\frac{1}{2}y$
Unit of commodity B	x	y

The facts represented in Table IV are precisely the same as those represented in Table III, though in Table IV the foreigner has the specious appearance of being more efficient, while in Table III it is the Englishman who has that appearance.

The reason why the same facts can be represented in either way is that no assumption has been made about whether the Englishman or the foreigner is, taking the two commodities together, the more efficient ; and the reason why no assumption was made is that it is irrelevant to the possibility of gain by interchange. This gain does not depend on the comparative cheapness of producing A in England and abroad or on the comparative cheapness of producing B in England and abroad. The gain depends on the relation between the ratio of the cost of production of A to that of B in England and the ratio of the cost of production of A to that of B abroad. *Gain is possible if the ratios are different.*

When trade is undertaken, the scene changes. Each country will come to produce more of some commodities and less or none of others. This will probably affect the costs of those which she still produces. New ratios of cost will be established. If these are still different from those prevailing abroad, gain can be secured by a further expansion of trade, and this again affects her ratios of cost. It follows that, when all the trade is undertaken that yields a gain, her ratios of cost will no longer be different from those abroad. A country should expand or curtail the production of different commodities until her ratios of cost are the same as those abroad, and export the surplus or import the deficiency so generated. (In some lines production may be abandoned entirely, and some goods may be imported which were not consumed, before trade was opened, owing to the excessive cost or impossibility of producing them at home.)

The principle set forth above is known as the Law of

Comparative Costs and is due to Ricardo. It remains the fundamental principle in this subject.

So far costs of transport have been neglected. Gain can only occur if (adopting the notation of Table III) the cost of sending a unit of B from England to its foreign market plus the cost of sending that amount of A which has the same exchange value as a unit of B from its source of production to England is less than y. Otherwise the saving in productive costs will be swallowed up by the additional costs of transport. Any reduction in the costs of transport enlarges the sphere of gain by foreign trade. To cost of transport, excess cost of salesmanship must be added, where by excess cost of salesmanship is meant the excess, if any, of the cost of selling a unit of English-produced B to its foreign buyer over that of selling it in England, plus the excess, if any, of the cost of selling the appropriate amount of foreign-produced A to the English buyer over that of selling it abroad. For the trade to yield net advantage, the saving in productive cost must exceed both the additional transporting and selling costs. Any improvement of diplomatic relations, any tightening of non-commercial bonds of intercourse between nations, or any increase of foreign investment, will probably make it easier for a seller to establish relations with his foreign market and so enlarge the sphere of possible gain by foreign trade.

§ 4. *A Calculation of the Gain from Foreign Trade.* The proposition that each country should produce what it can do most cheaply has now been defined. The next topic is the circumstances that determine the amount of gain which the trade yields. In the tables shown above, by " Cost of production in England " was meant the cost of producing that amount of the commodity which

England would produce if the channels of foreign trade were closed to her. By "Cost of production Abroad" was meant the cost of producing that amount of the commodity which would be produced abroad if there were no trade with England.

If England was a self-contained country the coal-wheat position might be illustrated by some such figures as :

TABLE V[1]

Costs in no-trade Condition.

	Cost in England.	Cost Abroad.
Unit of wheat . .	x	y
Unit of coal . .	x	$5y$

If in these circumstances interchange between England and the rest of the world becomes possible, costs can be saved if England produces some coal for export in exchange for wheat.

There are various possibilities with regard to the way in which costs will change as the scale of output is altered. In the cases of wheat and coal it is proper to suppose that the Law of Increasing Costs operates, that is, the larger the output the greater will be the cost of production per

[1] The reader will remember that this table does not profess to show the relation of the absolute cost of producing wheat abroad to that of producing it in England, or the relation of the absolute cost of producing coal. Actually, if England were cut off, the absolute cost of producing coal here would probably be somewhat less than abroad, while the cost of wheat would be very much higher. In the notation adopted *both* these facts are represented in the proposed figure of $5y$. (In this footnote the difficulty in principle of comparing absolute cost at home and abroad is neglected.)

unit. Reasons will be given subsequently for the view that this is the most general type of case.

As England increases her output of coal, her cost rises, and as she reduces her output of wheat, her cost falls ; and as the rest of the world increases its output of wheat, its cost rises, and as it reduces its output of coal, its cost falls. The new ratios might be as follows :

TABLE VI

Costs when some Trade is undertaken.

	Cost in England.	Cost Abroad.
Unit of wheat	$\cdot 8x$	$1\cdot 02y$
Unit of coal	$1\cdot 14x$	$4\cdot 986y$

The old ratios were 1 : 1 and 1 : 5. The new ratios are 1 : 1·4 and 1 : 4·9 (approximately). Since the ratios are still unequal and the Englishman has a comparative advantage in producing coal, something may be gained by his taking on the production of still more coal. He should push on with the production of coal until the rise in his cost of producing it and in the foreigner's cost of producing wheat and the fall in his cost of producing wheat and in the foreigner's cost of producing coal have brought the ratios of their costs to equality. Thus :

TABLE VII

Costs when full Trade is undertaken.

	Cost in England.	Cost Abroad.
Unit of wheat	$\cdot 25..x$	$1\cdot 075..y$
Unit of coal	$1\cdot 16..x$	$4\cdot 984..y$

Common ratio : $1 : 4\tfrac{7}{11}$

England is now producing a large quantity of coal for export and importing a large quantity of wheat. The ratios of the cost of production in the two spheres are the same, viz. precisely $1 : 4\frac{1}{11}$. Consequently no further gain can accrue by England taking over more production of coal.

First it is necessary to explain the figures chosen. Then an estimate of the gain due to the trade will be given. It should be remembered that this analysis relates to the potentiality of gain resulting from the international division of labour without reference to whether the actual course of trade is likely to follow this route.[1]

Cost figures in Tables VI and VII may be considered on the assumption that the aggregate output of wheat and coal is unchanged, the deficiency in the home output of wheat being made good by greater output abroad, and the extra home output of coal being compensated by reduced output abroad. The effect on demand is discussed subsequently. It will be observed that, as the output of wheat declines in England and rises abroad, the cost is made to fall in England by ten times as much as it rises abroad. Thus in Table VI the cost of wheat falls $\cdot 2x$ in England and rises $\cdot 02y$ abroad ; in Table VII it falls $\cdot 75x$ in England and rises $\cdot 075y$ abroad. Similarly the cost of coal rises first $\cdot 14x$ and then $\cdot 16x$ in England, and falls first $\cdot 014y$ and then $\cdot 016y$ abroad. These figures are reasonable and based on the simplest assumptions, provided that we suppose the pre-existent output in the rest of the world with which trade became available to have been ten times as great as that of England. For in that case the transfer of a given amount of output from

---

[1] The reader not interested in the details of this discussion may proceed direct to Section 11, *Conclusions*, page 40.

C

England to foreign lands involves a percentage change in the output of England ten times as great as the percentage change of output abroad.

Most commodities are produced, not in a single spot, but in a large number of different places, wheat-fields, mines, etc., each with its own law of increasing costs. If the output of foreign lands were ten times that of England, the simplest thing to suppose would be that there were ten times as many sources of output abroad as in England. In that case the average change in output from each source abroad would be one-tenth of the average change in output from each source in England when a given quantity of output is transferred between England and abroad. Every source may no doubt differ in the rate at which returns diminish when output is increased. Some will be able to expand with greater ease than others. It is fair to suppose in our initial illustration that England has the same share as the rest of the world of sources which can expand with normal ease, or which cannot expand without abnormal difficulty. With regard to a particular commodity there may be reason to suppose that this is not so ; for instance, it may be known that land in England is more highly cultivated than lands on the average elsewhere ; in that case English wheat sources would show returns diminishing on the average more sharply than those in the rest of the world. The effect of this on the gain by foreign trade receives examination below. We may retain our original assumption in all its simplicity for the present. In technical language it is that the gradient of the English cost curve is ten times as great as the gradient of the foreign cost curve. The rise in cost per unit of output is ten times as great in England ; the rise in cost for a proportional change of

output is, at the initial point, taken to be *equal* at home
and abroad. This is nearly but not quite the same as
making elasticity of supply equal at home and abroad.[1]

It is desirable to assess the gain which would accrue
from the interchange postulated in Table VII. To
explain the assessment is not a perfectly simple matter ;
but, since without it the whole aim and object of foreign
trade cannot be clearly grasped, the reader is asked to
follow patiently. England satisfies all her own demand
for coal, as she did before ; she satisfies some of her
demand for wheat and obtains the residue by producing
some extra output of coal which she exchanges for
wheat abroad. As she increases her output of coal its
cost per unit rises ; this is because she has to resort to
some poorer or less accessible fields. Making coal
subject to the Law of Increasing Costs implies that one
or more of the factors required to produce it cannot be
used equally well for the production of other things. If
that were not so, factors could simply be drawn from the
production of wheat to that of coal, and work alongside
those already engaged in the coal industry with equal
efficacy ; the production of coal could be extended
indefinitely in substitution for wheat without rising costs
per unit. As things are, coal-fields are a necessary factor,

---

[1] The gradient of the cost curve $\left(\dfrac{dy}{dx}\right)$ is an easier quantity to
handle in simple arithmetical examples than the elasticity
$\left(\dfrac{dx}{x} \div \dfrac{dy}{y}\right)$ and is therefore used in this exposition, at some small
sacrifice of logical requirements. If elasticity instead of
gradient were used, similar results would follow ; the change
of cost shown in the fourth term of the tables would be somewhat greater. The reader may safely substitute elasticity for
gradient in the *generalizations* of the text without error.

and good coal-fields are scarce. The extra coal has to be produced from inferior fields ; but the old coal also comes to cost more, for the increased output of coal involves a rise in the value of the good fields (one of the factors required to produce the " old " coal). What applies to coal applies to a wide variety of commodities, that require special facilities of production, whether land, special technique, proximity to raw materials, waterways, etc.

In assessing the gain from foreign trade, it is essential that we attribute to the coal produced for the home demand that cost of production which it had before the trade was opened, and no more. The increment of cost due to the higher value of the good coal-fields, whether going as higher royalties, profits, or even wages, to those engaged in them, is offset by the rise in the reward that these factors receive, and must not be counted in as an extra cost when we assess the national gain and loss from the trade. The apparent rise in cost is one method by which the gain is distributed. It may be taken therefore that England supplies her own demand for coal at the same cost as before. In assessing the cost of the extra output, the factors required for each extra unit should be entered at the value which they have when that amount and no more is produced.[1] The cost of the extra coal

---

[1] To compute the value of the factors at each stage, some one factor must be taken as a measure throughout. It is advisable to take some reasonable factor, such as a labour-day. But even if a most unreasonable factor, such as a given coal-field were taken, the same results would be deduced ; coal-mining might then appear not to be subject to increasing costs at all, but the rate at which wheat costs increased (decreased as production was curtailed) would be correspondingly enchanced, and the " ratio " would move in the same way as if another measure had been chosen.

thus rises from the original cost of x to the new cost of $1.16x$. The cost to the country of producing the extra coal per unit is thus something between x and $1.16x$; we may take the midway point, $1.08x$,[1] as the simplest assumption. By like reasoning the wheat, the production of which England abandons, used to cost $.625x$. Coal now exchanges for wheat at the rate of $1 : 4\frac{7}{11}$. Therefore the average cost, per unit, of the wheat obtained abroad by exchange with coal is $.233x$. England thus gets her wheat by trade at an average of 37.3 per cent of what it cost her to make it for herself. The productive resources so saved she may now expend in producing more coal to purchase additional wheat, or in producing more of other commodities, or she may enjoy greater leisure. By a like calculation it may be shown that the foreigner gets his imported coal at a saving of approximately 3.6 per cent.[2]

Table VII provides an example of an apparatus that may be used for computing the gain from trade in various circumstances. In order to obtain a clear understanding of the principles which may be deduced, the reader should make numerous experiments for himself.[3] The following sections contain some discussion of these principles.

§ 5. *Gain through Difference of Cost Ratios.* Gain by trade is possible when the cost ratios are different at home and abroad. It will be greater, the larger the difference is, other things being equal. This may be simply illustrated by tables constructed on the same plan as V and VII. In each country the wheat gradient is

---

[1] This assumes that the cost curve is a straight line.

[2] The sophisticated reader will perceive that in these two paragraphs I have had briefly to disentangle the truth from the fallacy in the proposition that "rent does not enter into the cost of production."   [3] See Appendix.

assumed to be equal to the coal gradient in these tables ;
when a certain amount of additional coal production is
undertaken in England, the quantity of wheat production
knocked off is taken to be equal to this amount multiplied
by the number of units of wheat at the ruling ratio that
can be obtained for a unit of coal. Consequently the
following rules are observed in the construction of all
these tables. Coal is made to rise in England by the
amount that wheat falls multiplied by the new ratio of
costs ; wheat is made to rise abroad by an amount equal
to its fall in England divided by 10, this coefficient
showing the size of the outer world compared with
England ; and coal falls abroad by the amount that
wheat rises there multiplied by the new ratio of costs.

Table VIII

Initial Position.

			Cost in England.	Cost Abroad.
Unit of wheat	.	.	x	y
Unit of coal	.	.	x	$10y$
Ratios	.	.	1 : 1	1 : 10

Table IX

When Full Trade is Undertaken.

			Cost in England.	Cost Abroad.
Unit of wheat	.	.	·12..x	1·088..y
Unit of coal	.	.	1·09..x	4·991..y
Common ratio	.	.	1 : $9\frac{2}{11}$	

The initial difference is bigger (foreign 1 : 10) than
that of Table VII (foreign 1 : 5). The final ratio (1 : $9\frac{2}{11}$)

is more favourable to England (Table VII, $1 : 4\frac{1}{11}$.)
Moreover the *volume* of trade on which gain is made is
greater. Since the cost gradients are supposed to be the
same as in Table VII, the volume of imports may be
inferred from the change in costs. The amount of wheat
imported is roughly $\frac{58}{78}$ times as great as that in the
conditions of Table VII.

The following tables give an example of a smaller
difference of ratios :

TABLE X

Initial Position.

			Cost in England.	Cost Abroad.
Unit of wheat	.	.	x	y
Unit of coal	.	.	x	$2y$
Ratios	.	.	. 1 : 1	1 : 2

TABLE XI

When Full Trade is Undertaken.

			Cost in England.	Cost Abroad.
Unit of wheat	.	.	$\cdot 630 . . x$	$1 \cdot 037 . . y$
Unit of coal	.	.	$1 \cdot 196 . . x$	$1 \cdot 98 . . y$
Common ratio	.	.	$1 : 1\frac{17}{22}$	

Here the final ratio is much less favourable to England.
Moreover the volume of imports is smaller, viz. $\frac{37}{78}$ths of
that secured in the conditions of Table VII.

§ 6. *Another Example of the Importance of being Unimportant.*[1] It appears at once from the figures of Table

[1] Cf. Henderson, *Supply and Demand*, ch. v, sec. 4.

VII that if the doors of foreign trade are thrown open
to a country, the gain to her is greater than the gain to
the rest of the world. In our illustration England got
her imported wheat in exchange for goods the cost of
production of which was but 37·3 per cent of what it
would have cost her to produce the wheat herself : the
foreigner got his coal from England at a cost of 3·6 per
cent less than that for which he could have produced it
himself. This does but confirm to common sense. If
Somerset were barred from trading with the rest of
England and the barrier were then lifted, the other
counties would doubtless gain by the fresh opportunities
for interchange, but the gain to Somerset would be
immensely greater. By like reasoning, if a particular
country reduced its tariffs—a partial barrier to trade—
the whole world would gain, but the gain to the particular
country would be far greater. It follows also that the
smaller the country, the more it is likely to gain by the
free interchange of its produce with that of other countries.

It must, of course, be understood that if a particular
country bulks very largely in the production of a particular
commodity, as England bulked in the production of
power-made goods a hundred years ago, or as Chile in
nitrates before the lowering in the cost of artificial nitrates,
the rest of the world may be an equal or even greater
gainer by the opening of trade with that country. This
may be seen if, in the former analogy, instead of Somerset,
all the coal-producing counties of England, or Lancashire,
had been supposed to be barred off.

Attention should be given in this connection to the
cost ratio in Table VII of $1 : 4\frac{1}{11}$. This is ten times
nearer the old foreign cost ratio ($1 : 5$) than it is to the
old English ratio ($1 : 1$); England gains accordingly.

If the outer world had been only twice as great as England, the cost ratio would have been $1 : 3\frac{2}{3}$, if 100 times as great $1 : 4\frac{97}{101}$, if equal to England $1 : 3$, etc.[1]

§ 7. *The Gain from Trade, and Cost Gradients.* Next we may consider the relation of cost gradients to profit by trade. In general it may be said that the less the cost gradients at home and abroad, the greater the gain from trade. But if England were very large, approaching half the size of the whole trading world, then it would be of advantage to her to have steeper cost gradients. England gains in all circumstances by low cost gradients in the outer world. But if England is of reasonable size, the elasticity of her own conditions brings in much greater gain than the elasticity of world conditions.

This may be illustrated by an adaptation of Table VII. It was assumed there that the cost gradient in England was proportional to that abroad. In Table XII it will be assumed that owing to the intense use to which her natural resources are put, or for other reasons, the cost gradient in England is twice as steep as was supposed in Table VII over the relevant range of output while that in the rest of the world is the same as in Table VII.

TABLE V (*Repeated*)

Initial Position.

		Cost in England.	Cost Abroad.
Unit of wheat	. .	x	y
Unit of coal	. .	x	$5y$
Ratios	. . .	$1 : 1$	$1 : 5$

[1] The formula by which these ratios can be calculated easily is given in the Appendix.

TABLE XII

Full Trade Position with English Cost Gradient twice that Abroad, in Proportion to her Size.

		Cost in England.	Cost Abroad.
Unit of wheat	. .	·24..x	1·038..y
Unit of coal	. .	1·158..x	4·992..y
Ratio	. .	1 : 4$\frac{17}{21}$	

Here a given transfer of wheat is seen to reduce the cost of production compared with the no-trade position in England by (·38×2)x, and to increase it abroad by ·038y; while an English increase of (·08×2)x in the cost of coal is balanced by a foreign decrease of ·008y. Thus the English cost gradient is proportionally twice as steep; the ratio of change in cost to percentage change in output is twice as great. What is the effect of this on the general position?

The first thing to notice about this table is that much less output is transferred. This may be seen at once by inspecting the cost abroad. Since the cost gradient is supposed to be the same abroad as in Table VII, the fact that the marginal cost of wheat abroad in Table XII only exceeds the cost when there is no trade by approximately half as much as it exceeds it in Table VII, and that the reduction in the cost of coal abroad is likewise approximately only half as great, indicates that there is only half as much transfer of production. Whatever gains may accrue from trade in the new situation, they will only come from a trade diminished by half compared with that envisaged in Table VII.

The final ratio of cost ($1 : 4 \cdot 8$ approximately) is, it is true, more favourable to England. (The ratio of Table VII was $1 : 4 \cdot 63 \ldots$). In Table XII wheat which England imports is cheaper relatively to coal which she exports, and this is a gain. The price which a country receives for her exports divided by the price which she pays for her imports (in this case the rate at which coal exchanges for wheat) is called her " real ratio of international exchange." This is more favourable to England in Table XII than Table VII. She gets more of what she imports per unit of her export.

Considering the same thing from another point of view, she gets her imported wheat for $\cdot 224 \ldots x$ units of cost,[1] while it would have cost her on the average $\cdot 62x$ to produce that for herself; thus she gets her wheat for approximately $36 \cdot 2$ per cent of the pre-trade cost; whereas on the assumption of Table VII she got it at approximately $37 \cdot 3$ per cent of the pre-trade cost.

But all this is a minor matter. The big change in the situation is that she imports far less wheat, approximately a half of the amount she would import in the conditions of Table VII. Of what importance is it that she gets what she does import at 36 per cent instead of 37 per cent of her own cost of production, when she is only importing a half of what she did in the other circumstances ? The fact that her costs are subject to sharper change as she alters the scale of output means that she gets into line with the world ratio of costs much more quickly, namely, approximately twice as quickly. Thus the smaller volume of trade due to the less elastic conditions of our second assumption limits the gain from trade far more than the improved ratio of interchange increases it. This springs

[1] Compare the calculation on p. 27.

directly from the fact of the world being a bigger place than the particular country.

J. S. Mill in his famous essay on The Laws of Interchange between Nations, has guided subsequent writers along a wrong path by considering elasticity with reference only to how it affects the ratio of interchange.[1] The more elastic the home supply the greater the volume of profitable trade for the country. The importance of this easily outweighs the fact that the more elastic the supply the less favourable will the ratio of international interchange be. A change in this ratio is always a bad indication by itself of improvement or deterioration in the foreign trade position.

Reflection unaided by numerical example may confirm the reader in his grasp of this principle. A country gains by foreign trade if and when the traders find that there exists abroad a ratio of prices very different from that to which they are accustomed at home. They buy what to them seems cheap and sell what to them seems dear. The bigger the gap between what to them seem low points and high points, and the more important the articles affected, the greater will the gain from trade be. If a change in the scale of production of the home country very materially alters her cost of production, so as quickly to bring it into line with foreign prices, the gain from trade is on a small scale, and is more or less fortuitous. But if when big changes are made in the scale of operations the comparative costs at home are altered

[1] His conclusions follow naturally from his postulate of two equipollent countries trading with each other. They would be relevant in an analysis of the effects of its bilateral tariff reductions, but irrelevant in that of the effects of unilateral or multilateral reductions.

little, that means that the fundamental economic structure of the country is such as to provide a permanent and solid basis for gainful trade. In this case the cost structure ruling when foreign trade is opened is not a transitory product of a variety of special causes, but is representative of the basic conditions of the country; and if this structure differs widely from the world structure, the scene is set for profitable operations on a large scale.

Turning to the conditions of supply abroad, we see that the lower the world cost gradient, the better for England, both because the lower the world gradient the greater the volume of profitable trade, and because the lower the world gradient the more favourable the ratio of interchange. Thus the country gains in two ways from a low world cost gradient; but the condition of the world cost gradient has a far smaller effect on the gain from trade than that of the home cost gradient.[1]

§ 8. *The Gain from Trade, and Demand.* The next point to be considered in connection with Table VII is its relation to the question of *Demand*. It was assumed that in equilibrium there was the same total output of wheat and coal, the foreign increase of wheat production merely offsetting the English decrease, and the foreign decrease of coal offsetting the English increase. Changes in demand were neglected.

It should be observed, however, that there was a certain reasonableness in the assumption of no change in aggregate output. The cost of wheat rises in the world by one-tenth of its fall in England and the cost of coal falls by one-tenth of its rise in England. If initially the output

---

[1] The reader may verify this by numerical examples for himself.

of each was ten times as great in the world as in England, as has been assumed throughout, and if the gradient of the demand for each is the same at home and abroad, the increase of demand for wheat at home should be equal to the fall abroad and the fall of demand for coal in England should be equal to its rise abroad. Thus the assumption of Table VII that the aggregate output of each was unchanged is consonant with the simplest assumption about demand at home and abroad, namely, that the gradient of each is in proportion to the size of the market.

When demand is taken into account, it appears that the volume of trade will exceed the volume of output transferred. The import of wheat will be equal to the reduction of the home output plus the increase of home demand. The export of coal will be equal to the reduction in foreign output plus the increase of foreign demand. This introduces a new factor in the estimation of gain from foreign trade. Some of the output of coal for foreign consumption is used to buy not the wheat which we no longer produce for ourselves but additional wheat which we could only have produced at a higher cost than x. Since the transfer of demand is voluntary the consumer's surplus on the additional consumption of wheat must exceed that on the consumption of coal sacrificed. Thus when demand is taken into account, the gain from foreign trade is seen to be greater than at first appeared.

The steeper the gradient of demand, the less the volume of trade will be. If demand were absolutely inelastic the volume of trade would be no greater than the volume of output transferred from one country to another. The lower the gradient of demand, the more the volume of trade will exceed the volume of output transferred, and the greater the quantum of trade on which the gain per unit is realized.

Thus, as in the case of supply, so in the case of demand, the lower the gradient the greater the gain. It is true that the lower the gradient of the home demand, the less favourable will be the ratio of international interchange. But if the outer world is very much larger than the home country, this disadvantage may be shown, by like reasoning to that used in the case of supply, to be small compared with the gain from the larger quantum of output exchanged.

§ 9. *Foreign Trade under Constant or Decreasing Costs.*

How does all this analysis apply, if the operation of the Law of Increasing Costs is no longer assumed ? In the first place it may be observed that its operation is by no means confined to the extractive industries. Technical skill, specialized managerial ability, adequate supplies of raw materials in proximity, and of power, in fact all the circumstances which make one country more fitted than another to produce particular commodities, are usually limited in their abundance. Constant or decreasing costs may possibly prevail over a certain range of output ; beyond it increasing costs are apt to supervene.

It is proper here to mention the class of costs, which simulate but are not identical with increasing costs of production, that Mr. Robinson has called costs of growth.[1] For purposes of this study the presence of these costs may be regarded as involving increasing costs of production ; an industry subject to them may ultimately be able to increase its exports without limit ; in an ordinary long period, expansion is limited by the rising

[1] Robinson, *Structure of Competitive Industry*, ch. VIII.

costs of growth; these like increasing costs proper serve to bring cost ratios in different countries to equality.

If the English production of B is subject to decreasing costs over a long range, but the drastic result of the whole world production being concentrated in England is not achieved, increasing costs ultimately supervening, the arguments of the earlier paragraphs apply. England gets benefits analogous to those which accrue when her cost gradient is very low, and the average cost per unit of increments of the commodity exported, calculated in the manner described above, may actually be *less* than the cost per unit of the original output. The gain from trade to England would be correspondingly enhanced.

If, however, constant and decreasing costs do persist indefinitely, so that the English ratio of A costs to B costs is never brought to equality with the world ratio, the production of A in England will be abandoned altogether. The rule that the ratios of costs within and without must be equal will apply in the negative sense, that there will be no inequality, since there will be no ratio in England. England will satisfy all her demand for A by exchanging B for it, at whatever the world ratio is after trade has been opened.

The pre-trade world ratio was, by hypothesis, more favourable to A than the pre-trade English ratio. If England got A in exchange for B at no better rate than the pre-trade English rate, she would gain by the trade by the amount that her cost of producing B has fallen. A fortiori, if she gets A at the pre-trade world rate she will gain. If decreasing costs prevail outside as well as inside England, the rate after trade has opened will be still more favourable to A. If on the other hand increasing

costs prevail in the outer world, the rate will be somewhat less favourable than the pre-trade world rate. It
will be more favourable, the larger the rest of the world
is compared with England.

§ 10. *A Multiplicity of Commodities Introduced.* In the
real world there are more than two commodities entering
into foreign trade. Inspection of A and B in isolation
(Table III)

TABLE III (*repeated*)

	Cost in England.	Cost Abroad.
Unit of A	x	y
Unit of B	x	$2y$

suggested that England should export B in exchange for
A. When other commodities are taken into account it
appears that this may not be desirable. For instance :

TABLE XIII

	Cost in England.	Cost Abroad.
Unit of A	x	y
Unit of B	x	$2y$
Unit of C	x	$5y$
Unit of D	x	$6y$
Unit of E	x	$10y$
Unit of F	x	$15y$

If these are all the commodities there are, it is certain,
assuming that transport costs are not excessive, that

D

England will export F and import A. That she will export B, as seemed likely when the veil was only drawn from two commodities, now seems extremely unlikely. Though England has an advantage in making B compared with A, she is at a disadvantage in B compared with C, D, E and F. Which, if any, of the commodities E, D, C and B, England will export depends on the importance of each and on the gradients of the supply and demand of each at home and abroad. All we can predict is that, if the maximum advantage of foreign trade is taken, the ratios in the two regions will be equal after trade has been opened and that this ratio will resemble the right-hand ratio of Table IX ($1 : 2 : 5 : 6 : 10 : 15$) more nearly than the left-hand ratio ($1 : 1 : 1 : 1 : 1 : 1$). It will resemble the right-hand more closely, the larger the outer world is, compared with the home country.

§ 11. *Conclusions.* (i) The leading principle of this chapter is that the gain from trade will be greater the more the ratios of the costs of production in England and abroad differ, when England and the rest of the world are cut off from one another. Relative improvement of productive efficiency in the outer world at producing the goods which we import redounds therefore to our advantage ; an improvement in making the goods which we export redounds to our disadvantage.

(ii) The bigger the rest of the world is relatively to ourselves, the greater the gain from trade. A general improvement in productive efficiency all round in the outer world, or a growth of population, redounds therefore to our advantage.

(iii) Any reduction in transporting costs or in the difficulty of selling in foreign markets or in the difficulty which a foreigner has in selling in our markets enlarges the possible sphere of gainful foreign trade.

(iv) The lower the gradient of the demand and cost curves over the relevant range of output, the greater the gain from foreign trade.[1]

These are the principal circumstances which determine whether and in what degree gainful foreign trade is possible. Our next question is—in what circumstances does the potentiality become an actuality ?

---

[1] This is true unless we approach the rest of the world in size, when it becomes advantageous for *us* to have steep cost and demand gradients.

CHAPTER III

POTENTIAL AND ACTUAL GAIN

§ 1. *Two Problems.* The last chapter was concerned with the fruits which can be reaped if the international division of labour is carried out on the right lines. It was an account of the direction which trade ought to take, or, what is the same thing, of the way in which countries ought to dispose of their productive resources.

The question which naturally seems to arise in succession to this is—do countries in fact tend to distribute their productive resources in this way and so gather in to the full the harvest which international division of labour is capable of yielding ? What is the mechanism which would allow them to do so ?

The answer which the classical writers gave to these questions was simple. Full advantage will in fact be taken of the international division of labour, if no artificial obstacles are put to the free flow of trade, if producers and merchants are allowed and encouraged to sell where they can get the highest price and buy where they find the lowest. It will be necessary to examine the presuppositions on which this simple answer rests.

Meanwhile there is another problem with which the classical economics did not concern themselves. The question which interested them was—what is the best way to distribute the employment of labour and other

42

productive services among different occupations ? There is the further question—what are the conditions in which these productive services will be fully employed ? It is now generally recognized that the volume as well as the nature of employment in the country is affected by international conditions. It will be necessary to explore the relation of the volume of employment to the international situation.

§ 2. *Three Conditions necessary for Maximizing Gain by Trade.* The present chapter is concerned with the first of these problems. It is convenient to confine the field of enquiry to the best employment of productive resources in any one country. What is said of one country will apply to each and every country and, so, to the world as a whole consequentially. Attention is also confined to the production of goods which are capable of being exported and imported and will in future be called tradable goods. The distribution of employment between tradable goods industries and other industries will be discussed subsequently.

If complete freedom of trade is allowed the prices of tradable goods in the country will not stand above their prices at any point outside by more than the cost of transporting them from that point to the country and the cost of establishing contact between the foreign seller and the domestic buyer, nor stand below their prices outside by more than the cost of carrying out the opposite operations. This condition, consequent upon free trade, may be called, briefly, the equality of prices at home and abroad.

It should be observed that, while this condition is consequent upon free trade, free trade is not necessary to it. For instance, if the whole of foreign trade was concentrated in the hands of an Export and an Import Board, they could arrange that it proceeded on the right lines. They would have to push exports and allow imports on such a scale that the ratios between the home costs of producing various commodities were equal to the ratios of the foreign offer prices on the frontier of competition wherever, in equilibrium, that frontier might be. In one respect this controlled system would allow greater latitude than the free trade system. The absolute level of prices at home might be higher or lower by any amount than the absolute level abroad, provided that equality in the ratios was secured. Unfortunately the proposers of this kind of control do not make it plain that this would be the basic principle guiding operations.

If the free trade condition is realized the two following conditions require also to be realized to secure the best international division of labour from the point of view of the country :

(i) The rewards charged by factors of production for services embodying a given degree of effort and skill must be the same in different occupations ;

(ii) Producers must be willing to push production of their various wares to the point at which the money costs of production are proportional to the prices which they can obtain.[1] If these two conditions are realized, the prices at which producers are willing to offer their various wares will be proportional to the real costs of production. If the free trade condition is also realized, the production of various wares will be pushed up to the

[1] These two conditions really reduce to one, if producers (or reproducers) are regarded as one factor of production.

point at which the ratios of the real costs of production of the various goods are equal to the ratios of the prices of the various goods in the world generally.

But we have seen that the best division of labour is secured if the ratios of the real costs of production are the same in different countries. This in turn will be secured if the producers in each country push production up to the point at which the real cost of production ratios are equal to the world price ratios. Things equal to the same thing are equal to one another. If the real cost ratios are in each country equal to the common price ratio, they will be equal to one another. And that is the condition for the best distribution of productive resources.

It may be observed that the prices of tradable goods in different countries are not, in the free trade conditions, absolutely equal, but may differ within the limits imposed by transporting and marketing costs. But precisely this difference between real cost ratios in the various countries was laid down in the foregoing chapter as being consistent with the best distribution of productive resources.

The two subsidiary conditions for the best utilization of productive resources are general, apply over the whole field of economics and are not in any sense special to the resources which enter into foreign trade. The direct proportion between the marginal utility in enjoying and the marginal disutility in producing various commodities, which in a money economy is achieved by making, price correspond to cost of production, is the general condition for the best distribution of productive resources among various occupations. Correspondence of price with real cost means that the factors of production are getting the same reward in different fields ; the consumer is paying them the same amount for their services whether they are making, say, boots, or motor-cars ; the marginal utility which the consumer is deriving from their services is the same in different fields ; no gain can therefore be made by transferring their services from one field to another. But if the rewards are different in different fields, higher, perhaps, in the production of cars than in that of boots, that is a sign that the marginal utility derived from a unit of service is higher in the case of cars than in that of boots, and that a gain could consequently be made by transferring some amount of service from the latter to the former until the rewards are reduced to equality.

A trade can only raise its rates of rewards above those of its neighbours by stinting the public of its services. Cannot it improve its relative position, it might be objected, by superior efficiency ? Certainly. Managerial skill and other forms of special skill must be counted among the factors. In the ideal equilibrium a trade conducted with higher managerial skill should show higher profit to the manager than those conducted with less. What the principle demands is that trades conducted with equal efficiency should show equal profits and rates of pay generally, and it is a platitude to remark that in the real world this is often not so. Whenever trades with equal efficiency show unequal rates of pay the public would gain by an increase in the scale of operations of one and a decrease in the other. If the rates of pay to all the factors are equal, the price, which is the sum total of the rewards to all the factors, must be proportional to cost.

A failure to adjust resources in this way necessarily means loss of national income, whether the commodities involved are those which enter into international trade or not. There is, therefore, no need to labour this principle further. A nation may be devoting too much attention to her exports or to some particular line of exports, or too little ; the test is whether wages and other rates of pay are below or above those prevalent elsewhere. When rewards in the unsheltered trades, as at the time of writing, are less than in the sheltered, it may be safely said that the amount of resources employed with the sheltered trades compared with that in the unsheltered is too small. At a time when productive resources are unemployed in all trades, it would be inappropriate to speak of a transfer of resources employed in one field to employment in the other. What can be said is that it is desirable that a larger proportion of the unemployed resources should be absorbed by the sheltered trades. Unfortunately a larger proportion are attached to the unsheltered trades. This has been, no doubt, a cause of the inadequate employment in both spheres.

§ 3. *Fulfilment of Conditions Abroad not Essential.* Since we are considering not the best distribution from the world point of view, but how any particular country can, taking the conditions in the outer world as given, best utilize her resources, the question of the conformity between the foreign cost structure and the world price structure becomes irrelevant. The best that a particular country can do for herself is to make her own price structure correspond to her own cost structure and to enter into such foreign trade as is consistent with that condition and with the prevailing world price structure. In a general way she gains and loses nothing by discrepancies between the world price structure and the world cost structure. That is the affair of the world ; each foreign country will be better off the less her own discrepancy is. The home country is indirectly concerned only in this way, that, according to the second conclusion of Chapter II, anything which makes the world richer will probably increase the benefits which she is in a position to derive from foreign trade.

The home country, viewing the prospects of foreign trade, is like the scientist studying nature. He is concerned with phenomena, with the external world as it impinges on his senses ; with changes of structure which can in principle have no effect on the world of experience, he has no concern. The trader's world of experience is the actual price structure of foreign countries.

Consider the case of what is call Dumping, the habit of selling abroad below the cost of production. Any habit which causes violent fluctuations in the foreign price structure certainly does affect the home country adversely. Each and every country is concerned to prevent situations in which producers find it profitable to make big changes in their selling prices, which have no relation to the long period trend. But in so far as the Dumping is a permanent habit, the home country can regard a sustained offer of goods by foreigners at prices below the cost of production, precisely as if the low price were due to low cost. The low price has the same effect on her whether the cause be low cost or policy.

If the Dumping has the effect of making the foreign price structure less like her own insulated cost structure, it is advantageous to her, if more like, disadvantageous. Roughly, the Dumping of goods upon her is likely to be advantageous, in that it enlarges the sphere of gainful foreign trade, while the Dumping of goods by competitors in her export markets is likely to be disadvantageous. Similarly, with regard to the products of foreign " sweated labour."

Foreign bounties or Protection have analogous effects. Protection to a particular commodity, while raising its price in the protected area, tends to make its open market world price fall. The goods which the output of the industries fostered by the foreign country displace have to find a market elsewhere or general production outside the protected area must be reduced. Both will probably happen. If this occurs in a commodity which the home country normally imports, she will gain, if in one which she normally exports, she will lose.

§ 4. *Failure of Conditions :* (a) *When Industries are Growing or Declining.* Free trade in conjunction with the two subsidiary conditions secures the best distribution of productive resources. In the following paragraphs something is said of the general circumstances likely to distrub the subsidiary conditions.

(i) Inequality of rewards in different occupations is a symptom that the transfer of productive resources from one trade to another is desirable. This may be due to a variety of reasons, a change in the world price structure, in the home demand, or in the technical efficiency of industries. The first sign that the transfer is desirable is a rise in the profits of the industry to which the transfer should be made or a depression in the profits of those from which it should be made, or both. The reward to the entrepreneurs in the two fields thus becomes unequal. This is necessary in a system of individualism to encourage entrepreneurs in one field and to discourage them in another. The greater the temporary disparity between profits, the more rapid is likely to be the transfer of attention from one field to the other.

It is sometimes thought that, owing to the sluggishness and conservatism of human nature, the natural incentive to shift is insufficient to make the shift occur as quickly as it is desirable that it should. This might be a reason for increasing the incentive artificially by giving bounties or Protection to the prosperous industry. It constitutes a part of the argument for protecting Infant Industry, an argument directly opposed to the recent British policy of safeguarding, which sought to give artificial support to industries in a state of natural decline. The policy here suggested is to foster the strong in order to accelerate their growth and squeeze out the weak more rapidly.

Against this it may be urged that there is danger in such a policy, since time is required to show whether the change in circumstances which engendered the prosperity is to be permanent. A reckless transfer of resources to and fro would be wasteful. The tardiness of entrepreneurs may not be more than prudent caution requires. It should also be remembered that profit derived from the use of existing plant is sheer gain and that, so long as liquid resources used in conjunction with the plant are earning their proper rate of reward, the plant should continue to be exploited. The low rate of profit is naturally a grievance to the owners of the plant. Nothing should be done to assist these owners, since their plight is part of the mechanism by which production is transferred to the right industries in an individualist system.

While profits are high in one field and low in another,

pressure may be brought to bear to alter wages and salaries, by the wage-earners in one case and by the entrepreneurs in the other. If this is carried out, a discrepancy between comparative real costs and comparative prices arises, the money costs in the prosperous field are higher and in the depressed field lower in proportion to the cost in terms of the amount of the factors of production used. While this disparity exists. the weak trade is artificially fostered and allowed to drag out its declining career longer than it otherwise would. This discrepancy represents a further failure to make an immediate transfer of productive resources to their most profitable point of operation. If low wages are in the export trades, unprofitable foreign trade is being maintained in the wake of opportunities of profit now vanished, if in the internal trades, insufficient advantage is being taken of the opportunities in the foreign field.

The shifting of rates may be due to the prevalence of a good level of employment in the prosperous field and of unemployment in the depressed one. If there is an actual shortage of hands in the good field the shift may be desirable as being the only method of stimulating the transfer of workmen. It is analogous to the shift in comparative profits.

It might be urged that even in these circumstances the shift in rates is a sign of undesirable sluggishness on the part of the wage-earners, on the ground that the mere offer of employment in the improving field should be enough to attract the unemployed from the depressed occupation. But a change of occupation has its sacrifices and, if that is so, it is not desirable to make the change unless there is an increment of income to compensate for those sacrifices. If in these circumstances a shift in wage rates is necessary to induce the change, while the discrepancy lasts the nation is losing in production, since the high price asked by the prosperous trade to cover high wages is unduly restricting the home or foreign demand for its wares, and the low price which the depressed trade is able to ask unduly expands the demand for its ; but this loss is offset by the saving of sacrifice in the troublesome and painful process of transfer, which, it maybe, can be conducted with a smaller aggregate of disutility in leisure than in haste.

A discrepancy of wage rates when there is unemployment in both fields seems less easy to justify. It is only justifiable at all in so far as it stimulates transfer. But a relatively high wage rate in the prosperous field, combined with some measure of unemployment, is hardly likely to act as a strong stimulus. A relatively high rate of reward for any factor in an occupation is justified so long as there is a shortage of the factor there, both as a necessary check to the demand for the commodity and an attraction inducing more of the factor to come from elsewhere. But, if there is unemployment in that field in addition to that due to normal seasonal fluctuation or the shifting of employment between various firms, the higher rate is probably objectionable.

Broadly, in the world at large, there has for some time been, and will continue to be, a shift away from agriculture. The reason for this is, as Mr. Loveday has so well shown,[1] that as people grow rich they spend a smaller proportion of their income on food. The capacity of the stomach is limited. The amount of food consumed continues to increase, but it increases at a lower rate than that of other commodities. If the birth rate among

[1] *Britain and World Trade, passim.*

agriculturists is not lower than the average, men must be continually dragged out of agriculture into other occupations. This has been to some extent offset in the past by the slower rate at which productive efficiency in agriculture has increased, but with modern methods this increase will be speeded up. Consequently there has been a tendency for agricultural wages, at least in the old countries, to stand permanently below those of manufacturing industry—for the shift over is a continuous one. Thus agriculture is permanently stimulated to produce more than its correct output, by the comparative bounty to it provided by the low wages prevalent in it. There is thus a prima facie case for giving some compensating artificial stimulus to manufacturing industry in general, especially in countries which are not already encumbered by an intense manufacturing development. In countries which are, it is believed, reasonably or unreasonably, that it is desirable to keep a certain proportion of the population on the land and that this outweighs the gain which would be derived from further industrialization.

If the shift away from agriculture required for the proper distribution of productive resources in the world becomes larger, the discrepancy between rewards in agriculture and those elsewhere will increase also. In the upward phase of the trade cycle secular movements of decline are usually lost sight of, while they are accentuated in the downward phase. A crisis in agriculture and a collapse in agricultural prices may be expected to be regular features of the downward phase of the trade cycle in future, unless some other means be found for securing a quicker shift over in productive resources, or the trade cycle be eliminated.

The production of raw materials is likely to have a similar fate. Increased wealth not only involves an increase in the bulk of raw materials used but also an increase in the degree to which they are worked up. This in turn means that a larger proportion of mankind will be needed for the finishing processes. Technical improvements in the utilization of raw materials may lead in the same direction. The production of consumable necessities may yield to that of quasi-luxuries. Within the sphere of quasi-luxuries there will be much more shifting about of demand than in the old more indigent days. The last-mentioned type of shift, however, is different from the others we are discussing, since its consequences are transitory and irregular. The shifts from one broad class, such as foodstuffs or raw materials, to another are enduring and likely to set up permanent discrepancies between rates of pay in different occupations. These discrepancies, which, for short, we may call wage discrepancies, have an appropriate effect in stimulating the transfer of labour and an inappropriate effect in limiting the transfer of enterprise. Whether they should be encouraged or discouraged depends on the circumstances of the case, on how necessary and effective they are in the matter of producing the movement of labour. In so far as they are judged necessary there is a case for giving an offsetting artificial inducement to the producers who are engaged in the growing branches of industry, and for giving an additional squeeze to those who are being squeezed out by the natural progress of events.

§ 5. *Failure of Conditions :* (b) *Monopoly.* (ii) Prices may fail of adjustment to comparative real costs, because the factors have opportunities for organizing themselves better in one occupation than another, and so for securing better rates of reward. Discrepancies arising for this reason are wholly injurious, in that they deflect the employment of productive resources from the right channels.

(iii) Prices may also fail of adjustment to comparative real costs, because the monopolistic or quasi-monopolistic character of a certain industry enables the employers to hold prices above costs. This circumstance may not be unconnected with the disparities in wage rates mentioned in paragraph (ii) above, the men being able to stand out for higher rates in the quasi-monopolistic trades. Classical writers on economics were in the habit, when discussing monopoly, of dismissing it as an exceptional phenomenon. This attitude is out of date for two reasons, first because of the great growth in recent years of monopolistic combinations of various kinds, whether mergers, trusts, cartels or gentlemen's agreements, and secondly because the theoretic analysis of monopoly and competition has revealed that both monopoly and competition are limiting concepts, abstractions, relating to conditions not always realized in practice, and that most industries work in conditions which are an admixture of those represented by the two concepts. Thus a large sphere which the classical writers thought of as competitive is in fact only so in a partial sense.

The ideal of competition tends to be realized in the case of completely standardized commodities in which the market is fully organized and the individual producers many and unorganized. In this case an individual throws his produce on the market in the confident expectation that he will get the ruling price for it and that his contribution will not have a discernible effect on that price.

E

It is in his interest to push his production up to the point at which its cost is equal to the prevailing price.

True monopoly, on the other hand, is realized when a single firm, by the possession of a state grant or patent, or of the whole of the available supplies of a limited natural product, or in virtue of its immense size and commensurate resources, which enable it easily to buy off any competitor who is not prepared to operate on a similar scale, has absolute control over the whole market. Such a firm pushes its production not to the point at which its cost is equal to the price, but only to the point at which its cost is equal to the increment of receipts due to the marginal product.[1] The price exceeds the increment of receipts in the case of the monopolist, for, since he is the sole supplier, a discernible increase of his output has a discernible effect on the market price. It will depress the market price by an amount which depends on the elasticity of demand. But this depression in the price affects the whole of the rest of his output. By increasing his supply he has spoilt his own market. The increment of receipts due to this extra output is not the price of this increment of output at the new price level, but the price of this less the difference between the price at which he used to sell the rest of his output and the price at which he now has to sell it. He will not produce this extra output unless the increment of receipts, so measured,

[1] For industries subject to decreasing costs, marginal cost must be substituted for cost in this sentence ; total cost per unit will be somewhat higher than marginal cost, but it will still stand below the price, if the quasi-monopoly allows abnormally high profit to be made. (Total cost per unit, or, as more briefly expressed in the text throughout, cost, is taken to include a normal rate of profit for the entrepreneur.)

which is due to it, covers the cost of making it.   The price
exceeds the increment of receipts and consequently cost
the more, the less elastic the demand.   The monopolist
is always limited in his attempt to mulct the consumer by
the elasticity of demand.   Happily the demand for most
commodities has a considerable degree of elasticity owing
to the availability of substitutes.   Traffic may desert the
railways and take to the roads ; electricity may be used
instead of gas, etc.

Few producers have an absolute monopoly ; but less
producers than used to be supposed work in conditions
of ideal competition.   Any condition in which a producer cannot increase sales without making a price
concession implies partial monopoly.   This may arise in
two ways, either by adhesion to an agreement among the
producers, or because the market is not completely
organized or the product not standardized.

In both these cases price will stand above the increment
of receipts due to an increment of output.   But the
cost will be equated, so far as the producer's knowledge of
his own cost and market conditions enables him to equate
it, to the increment of receipts.[1]   Consequently the price
will stand above the cost of production.   Producers will
often fail to act in their true interest, but we may assume
that their efforts to do so will lead to an even distribution
of their errors around the point of their true interest, and
the principle that the cost shall be equal to the increment
of receipts, if not verified in the case of each individual,
may be accepted as a statistical law.

Under this head the discrepancy between price and
cost will be greater, the more important the element of

[1] For the modification required in this proposition in the
case of decreasing cost industries, *vid.* p. 56, footnote.

goodwill, the more specialized and individual the product
and the less organized the market. The greater the
discrepancy, the more output will fall below the level
required if productive resources are to be distributed
in the right way.

Whether anything can be done to whip these partial
monopolists into greater activity in an individualist
economy is a question difficult to answer.

§ 6. *Summary*. To resume the main thread of argument.
In Chapter II it was laid down that, to gain full advantage
of international division of labour real cost ratios
must be the same in all countries. In the present
chapter it has been argued that the most any particular
country can do is to make her real cost ratios correspond
to world price ratios.

This correspondence will be effected if three conditions
are realized.

(i) The price ratios must be the same inside as outside
the national frontiers (the Free Trade condition).

(ii) Rewards to factors must be the same in different
occupations.

(iii) Producers must be prepared to sell their wares
at prices proportional to the money costs of production.

Something has been said of the general circumstances
which are likely to cause a failure of the second and
third conditions.

CHAPTER IV

COMPARATIVE PRICE LEVELS

§ 1. *A Classification of Goods.* In Chapter III two questions were put. One, dear to the heart of classical economists, was, what is the best distribution of a nation's productive resources among different occupations? The other was, what are the circumstances in which a nation will be able to make full use of her productive resources? Before the second question can be answered some consideration must be given to the relation of national price levels to each other. For the purpose of this study it is convenient to make a three-fold classification of goods. The division sketched out below has, like all such divisions, an arbitrary element. Many similar divisions might be made. In the attempt to analyse a highly complex phenomenon some arbitrary simplification is inevitable.

A. The first division of goods, called briefly A goods hereafter, are the staple goods of homogeneous character and capable of entering into foreign trade. This class consists in the main of raw materials and foodstuffs. The rates at which such goods exchange for each other are, with due allowance for the costs of transport, common throughout the world. Gold is such a commodity. If we take price to be the exchange value measured in terms

59

of gold, these goods have a single international price level. The prices of silver, copper, corn of specific quality, rubber, tea, etc., are telegraphed from market to market and, if the price of an ounce of silver in London differs from its price in New York by more than the cost of transporting that ounce one way plus that of transporting its price in gold the other, that difference is at once corrected by an arbitrage operation. If the price of silver is higher in London, it is simultaneously offered for sale in London and purchased in equal quantity in New York, until its price is brought to an equality in the two centres. The same is true of all staple goods for which an organized market exists in the important commercial centres throughout the world.

The conditions of perfect competition referred to on pp. 55–56, have, on the whole, tended to prevail in the production of A goods. But deliberate attempts at the control of output by producers' agreements have recently been made in a large number of cases.

B. When much labour is embodied in the working up of raw materials into a finished or half-finished condition, the resulting commodities are apt to be somewhat specialized in character, differing in quality and detail of design according to the place in which the manufacturing process is carried out. These differences destroy the unity of the world market. English electrical apparatus designed for a certain purpose may be different in various particulars from German electrical apparatus designed for the same purpose. Consequently machinery for organizing a single world price for such apparatus cannot come into play. Each type of product has its own price. The difference between such prices is often greater than the qualitative differences of the products might be expected to justify. An organized market establishes an impersonal contact between those who have a demand for and those who have a supply of the commodity there dealt in. In the absence of such a market, the contacts are of a more personal kind, good-will is established between buyer and seller, channels of trade become stereotyped, habits are formed and the substitution of German goods for similar English goods can only be secured by a bigger price differential than that corresponding to the difference in the utility of the goods.

To this category of goods many services also belong. Insurance or the issue of securities ought, it might be thought, to be susceptible of international standardization. But many differences in the detail of national law and custom creep in, to distinguish the quality of the services offered at various commercial centres. In consequence of this firms can establish relations of goodwill with their clients, habits are formed, and an international unity of market is not achieved.

C. Some goods and services are by their nature incapable of entering into international trade. Such are houses, fixed plant, railway services, public utility services, and domestic services ; these cannot be moved from their location.

Retail goods must in general be regarded as amalgams of A (or B) and C goods. This fact has important implications, as will subsequently appear. The price of coal to the domestic consumer is, it is well known, very much higher than its price at the pit-head. The prices of all goods in the shop window stand well above the prices at which those goods are discharged from the factory. The difference is due to the many services which have to be performed in transporting the goods and making them available for the retail purchaser's selection. If the goods were to be exported, such services would be irrelevant. When the goods reach the shop window they must be regarded as embodying a purely domestic (C) element ; they would only be capable of being exported at a value far below that which they are now expected to have attained ; they have been metamorphosed from tradable into non-tradable goods.

There is no international price level for Class C goods. The price levels of these goods in different countries are related to each other only through the relation of each to the A and B goods.

We have then before us the following problems :

(i) What determines the international price level, that is, the common world price level of A goods ?

(ii) What determines each national price level of C goods ?

(iii) B goods stand in an intermediate position. There is some tendency towards a common international price level. But complete uniformity is seldom achieved and for long periods there may be considerable differences between the prices of similar B goods of different national origin.

The discussion of this chapter presupposes some common world monetary standard, such as gold. The complications which arise when various countries have independent standards must be postponed, until the monetary mechanism has been explored.

§ 2. *The Price Level of International Goods.* The traditional treatment of monetary theory is not wholly satisfactory for the study of international trade. This treatment uses the concept of a general price level, which is the reciprocal of the value of gold. The general price level can thus be shown to depend on the demand and supply of gold, which in turn depends, when allowance has been made for its industrial uses, on the quantity of valuables it has to be exchanged against, on the rapidity with which it is turned over, and on its quantity. The equation embodying this truth, which is known as the quantity theory of money, may then be set out.

The validity of this theory cannot be shaken, but its employment is not of great service in the elucidation of the problem before us. If it is applied on a world scale, it determines, not the international price level, that is, the average of the prices of A goods which have a common international price, but the *general* world price level, which must include the prices of all valuables exchanged and, in particular, of samples of B and C goods from all nations. The quantity equation applied on a world scale does not bring out the relation of the international price level to the national price levels.[1]

The international price level does depend partly on the relation of the quantity of gold and its efficiency in use to the world output of goods. But it also depends on the relation of the demand and supply of world goods to the aggregate demand and supply of all national (C) and quasi-national (B) goods. It is sometimes rashly assumed that, if the production of gold were sufficient to keep pace with the increase in the world production of goods, the international price level would remain steady. But

[1] For the variety of different price levels and the equations appropriate to each, see J. M. Keynes, *Treatise on Money*, chs. IV–VI

this would not occur if the value of these goods happened to decline, as it probably will over a long period, for reasons stated in Chapter III, relatively to a sample of all national goods. Even if the production of gold were sufficient, which it probably will not be, to keep pace with the increased world production of goods, the international price level would probably fall. This, conjoined with a rise of other price levels, might be accepted as a necessary evil, but its incidence on the burden of international debts should be noticed. Since these can only be paid in international and quasi-international (B) goods,[1] the burden of international debts, payable with relatively depreciating assets, must increase, even if the general value of the gold in which they are expressed were held stable.[2]

The unity of the international price level is disturbed by transport costs and broken by tariffs. In the case of A goods, a traveller leaving a centre of output will ascend a slope of rising prices until he reaches the watershed which bounds the area supplied by a neighbouring centre. The level at the various centres is not necessarily the same. The price at each centre plus the cost of transport to the watershed dividing them, must be the same. If the gradient of the ground (i.e. the cost of transport per mile) is the same on either side of the watershed, the price will be lower at whichever of the centres is further

[1] Also called above quasi-national goods. These terms are clearly interchangeable.

[2] The *real* burden will not increase if the reason for the relative fall of A goods is a relative increase of efficiency in producing them ; but it will increase in so far as the fall is due to the sluggishness of factors in transferring themselves to the production of goods for which there is a relative rise in demand.

from the watershed. Generally prices will tend to be low near the large centres of supply. But quite small centres may reach very low levels if the gradient in the neighbourhood is steep. Small centres may also be found at very high levels. The demand may be thought of as being drained into the centres of supply, lakes whose sizes depend on the amount of the demand which they satisfy.

Tariffs are dams impeding the flow of demand outwards from a given area (but not impeding the flow, if there be one, in the contrary direction). If some of the demand flows out over the dam, the price inside will exceed that outside by the amount of the tariff. If, however, the tariff is completely obstructive, the price inside may stand anywhere between the price outside plus the tariff and the price outside. The price immediately inside the dam cannot fall below the price immediately outside it, for it does not obstruct the inward flow of demand.

§ 3. *The Price Level of Quasi-International Goods.* A traveller exploring the price level of B goods finds somewhat different scenery. In the first place the ground is rougher, partly because tariffs are more numerous and higher, but also because the market is incompletely organized and the cost of salesmanship is heavier. Different prices for very similar goods may be found in close geographical proximity, if trade is running in old channels. The margin of a centre's market may not be the most distant part of it. One feature may strike him particularly. In the case of A goods he found that, as he approached a centre, prices fell to a minimum in its immediate vicinity. In the case of B goods he may find an opposite phenomenon—prices rising as he approaches the centre of supply. He is then in the presence of the notorious and unduly maligned practice of dumping. The centre of supply will in this case prove to consist, not of a large number of independent competitors, but of a single firm or group of firms with a tacit or expressed agreement to exploit the market to the best of their advantage. They can charge a higher price near the centre of their area because that is most distant from the rival centres. In pure competition it is only to consumers in close proximity to the watershed that it is nearly a matter of indifference which centre they draw their supplies from; to those much nearer one centre than another it is a great advantage to draw from their own centre. The monopolist or quasi-monopolist exploits this advantage and extracts a higher price from his immediate neighbours than he gets from those on the periphery.

For this reason a country which exports more B goods than she imports is likely to have a higher general price level than the country which imports more B goods than she exports. For, since we may suppose such a country to import more A goods than she exports, the price level of the A goods will probably be higher than that of the country in the opposite position, to cover the higher cost of transport of the A goods; the price level of her B goods, on the other hand, will not be proportionately lower and may not be lower at all.

From the nature of the contours the traveller may get some glimpse of the future. If high and low priced B goods of similar quality are selling side by side, the high priced centre is only maintaining its position by a good-will, that is bound to wear down with time. The area controlled by the centre supplying the high priced B goods is probably subject to a long period recession.

Another rough generalization may be made about the B goods price level. In a period of falling world demand and a falling general price level, the production of goods will tend to be cut down. Suppose that there is no general fall in the reward to factors of production. In the case of A goods the law of increasing costs comes into play and the lower world prices are met by a restriction of production which reduces their real cost. B goods are more generally subject to the law of decreasing costs over a wide range on the productive side. A restriction of output may have no tendency to reduce real costs. It will therefore have to be pushed further if the new price is to cover the cost. If there is no reduction in rewards, the price of B goods will be sustained and the fall in demand will have to be met by a sufficient restriction of output. The A industries will complain chiefly of over production and low prices in the slump, while the B industries will complain of excess capacity and unemployment ; output will be more sharply restricted in the latter and the price level better sustained.

§ 4. *The Price Levels of Domestic Goods.* It is now necessary to approach the problem of the relation of the national price levels of C goods to the international price level of A goods. The class of C goods as originally defined includes the fixed capital of the country. The following remarks do not apply to the price of existing capital equipment, but only to that of new equipment (of kinds that cannot be exported) as well as to all C services such as transportation, retailing, catering, public utility services, etc.

Any two countries will tend to have the same price of C goods if the three following conditions are fulfilled. If these conditions fail, the price level of C goods will be unequal in the two countries.

It should be remembered that the goods falling into this class differ according to the tastes and habits of different countries, and difficulties of detail arise in any attempt to measure the price levels against each other. This analysis only aims at a broad result.

(i) The ratio of the efficiency in producing C goods to that in producing A goods must be the same in the two countries.

(ii) The rewards to factors of production must either be the same in A industries as they are in C industries in each country, or the ratio of the rewards in A industries to those in C industries must be the same in both countries. (The former of these alternatives is a special case of the latter.)

(iii) The average excess of price over money cost, if any (this being due to monopolistic or quasi-monopolistic conditions among producers), in respect of C goods must bear the same relation to the excess of price over money cost, if any, in respect of A goods in both countries.

With regard to the first condition, it may be observed that great differences between national levels of efficiency are usually due either to differences in natural resources or to difference in the degree to which scientific knowledge and capital have been applied to manufacturing processes. Both these differences affect the production of A and B goods. On the side of retailing, transport and domestic service it is doubtful if differences in efficiency occur on so great a scale. Since gold rewards are proportional to efficiency in the output of tradable goods, highly efficient countries may find the gold cost of providing their C services, in which proportional economies cannot be made, higher than that in the less efficient countries. It may be expected, therefore, that the price level of C goods will be higher in the more efficient countries. Experience confirms this theoretic conclusion.

The cost of living is compounded of the prices of A, B and C goods. The efficient countries will therefore tend to have a high cost of living.

If the second condition is not fulfilled and rewards in the sheltered industries exceed those in the unsheltered industries by more in one country than another, the output of the sheltered industries will, *ceteris paribus*, be more highly priced in the former country.

The popular idea that in times of change there will be greater pressure to adjust rewards to factors in the unsheltered (A and B) industries than in the sheltered (C) industries is well founded. Whereas a period of slump involves some contraction in the demand for C goods and therefore some pressure to reduce rewards, a fall in the world price level of A and B goods may leave a country, whose rewards remain stationary, high and dry, in the sense that none of its A and B products could be marketed at all if costs had to be covered at the old level of rewards.

While the tendency to equality of the price levels of A goods and, within broader limits, of B goods in different countries is indisputable, it cannot be said that there is such a tendency in respect of goods in general. On the contrary, a general equality of prices in which C goods— and all retail goods have an important C element—are included would only be realized in special and unlikely circumstances.

If countries have, as has been assumed hitherto, a

common monetary standard, such as gold, prices may be compared directly. If there is no common standard, prices in each country are expressed in terms of different national units and must be measured against those in other countries by reference to the rates at which the national currencies exchange with each other.

Whatever the rates of exchange ruling, the prices of A goods, so measured, will not vary outside the limits imposed by the costs of transport and tariffs.

If countries have no common monetary standard, fluctuations may occur in the rates at which their currencies exchange against each other. Some of these fluctuations may be caused by transient day-to-day conditions. An attempt has been made to distinguish such fluctuations from those due to the normal trend by reference to comparative national price levels. This attempt is known as the Theory of Purchasing Power Parity. It is asserted that the rate at which currencies exchange against each other should normally be that rate which causes each when converted into the other to purchase the same quantity of goods in the land of the currency into which it has been converted as it purchases at home. That the purchasing power may diverge within the limits imposed by the cost of transport and tariffs is recognized.

If attention is confined to A goods, it is clear that currencies converted at the ruling rates of exchange will purchase the same quantity of these, whatever the rate of exchange. For as quotations are telegraphed from centre to centre, each centre calculates the rate at which it will quote for A goods by taking the rates, at which the currencies of each centre exchange, into account. In each country A commodity prices are purely the effect of the foreign exchange rate and cannot be used to determine what that rate of exchange should normally be.

When C goods are taken into account the Theory of Purchasing Power Parity is no longer true. For C goods are not expected to have the same prices in different countries, except in the unusual case in which the three conditions referred to above are fulfilled. If the degree of failure of actual conditions to correspond to those postulated were known and could be accurately measured, it would be possible to deduce the normal rate of foreign exchange from the actual prices of C goods. The normal rate of exchange must correspond to purchasing power parity after the failure of these conditions to be realized has been taken into account. If a simultaneous shift occurs both in the normal rate of exchange and in the degree of failure of these conditions to be realized, whether the latter shift is necessarily cause and the former effect, or whether the rôles may be reversed, we are not yet in a position to consider. We can only do so after a study of the monetary system.

§ 5. *The Price Levels of Factors of Production.* Factors of production are like C goods in that there is no tendency towards a common international price level. Uniformity of price level is brought about by the free flow of demand from a high to a low level and the flow of goods in the opposite direction. Some of the factors are completely immobile, between nations, others have a very limited degree of mobility. Mines, land, railways and fixed equipment cannot be moved at all. There is some international flow of labour, but a very small one relatively to the large wage differences which exist. Migration is impeded by the cost of movement, by the many sacrifices

F

which the severance of home ties and the abandonment
of well-tried habits of life involve and, especially in
recent times, by severe national restrictions on immigra-
tion.   South America is the only important region of
the world which can be said to welcome immigrants. The
movement of scientific knowledge, business ability, and
industrial skill is also extremely slow and sticky. Free
capital moves somewhat more easily. Foreign investment in fixed interest securities is restricted by the
possibility that the lending or borrowing country may
depart from the gold standard, and by the investor's
ignorance of the chances of default owing to political or
economic distrubances in the borrowing country. Other
forms of foreign investment are also restricted by the
investor's ignorance of the true prospect of the success
of enterprises in distant lands. International movement
of free capital on a large scale does nevertheless occur.

Classical writers made the immobility of factors of
production the basis of the division between their treatment of national and that of international trade. Within
the country it was assumed that rewards to factors in
different employments might legitimately be regarded as
tending to equality. As between different countries this
is not even an approximation to the truth.[1] In a closed
national system the proper distribution of productive
resources among occupations is that which makes the
output in each have equi-marginal utility. To secure
equi-marginal utility of output in the world as a whole,
the factors of production would have to be moved from
one nation to another on a vast scale. The output of
productive resources in the U.S.A. or England has
exceeded and will long continue to exceed the output in

[1] Cf. ch. I, sec. 3.

Poland or India. To secure the best international division of labour with the existing distribution of population and skill, it is necessary to fall back on the principles already enunciated. Goods should be allowed to flow between countries so as to secure that the *ratios* of the output per head in different occupations should be approximately equal in all countries. The *absolute level* of output must remain different in different countries, so long as the factors of production cannot flow freely between them. The countries which have the higher absolute level are the more efficient countries.

Broadly, rewards to factors in each country are in proportion to their efficiency. The substantial truth as well as the limitations to this doctrine may be demonstrated by supposing the opposite. In what follows it is assumed that the relation of prices to costs in the world as a whole is such that productive resources in the world generally are in reasonably full employment. The opposite condition receives examination in a subsequent chapter (Ch. VIII), but is not relevant to a consideration of the relative position of countries. First suppose rewards in a particular country to be low in relation to her efficiency. Rewards may be apparently but not really low in this sense. For instance, low wages per hour may so impair the health and efficiency of wage-earners, that a rise would increase output per unit of wage cost. To raise wages above such a level would be to make them lower " in relation to the efficiency of the country," and conversely. If rewards are low, the prices which a country can obtain by the sale of her A and B goods will then on the average exceed the rewards payable to her factors in respect of their productive services. But this is impossible. The price received for a commodity must be divided among factors of production. It follows that the sum total of rewards payable in respect of a representative parcel of her output cannot be less than the price obtainable for it.

A distinction may, however, be drawn between the relatively inflexible rewards to factors, whose rate is pre-determined by contract or agreement, and the adjustable item of profits. The sum total of inflexible rewards may be low in relation to the efficiency of a country, profits being correspondingly high. If this condition persists pressure may be brought to bear to raise the inflexible rewards. In accordance with the general theory of value, each factor will be rewarded in proportion to its own marginal net product. It should be observed in passing, however, that if one of the factors, such as labour, is not well organized to press its claim for a rise in reward when occasion offers, it may, in certain circumstances, continue for a long period to be paid a reward which is low in relation to the productive capacity of the country, it may continue, so to say, to be " exploited " ; the certain circumstances may be defined as those in which employers are in a quasi-monopolistic condition *vis-à-vis* labour. This, in its turn, may be explained as the condition, which is indeed the usual one in the absence of collective bargaining, in which a rise in the demand price of labour does not operate through an organized market, but is volunteered by an employer. An employer who offers such a rise has to pay more not only for the increment of labour he may wish to take on, but for all the labour he is already employing, and tends to make the marginal product of labour equal not to the wage he pays, but to the total increment of outlay in which the rise of wages required to attract the marginal increment of labour involves him.[1] Wages will then stand below the marginal net product of labour.

Secondly, suppose that rewards are high in relation to the efficiency of the country. At first sight this might also appear to be impossible since not more than the price obtained for the representative parcel of products can be paid out to factors. Inflexible rewards might indeed be high, profits in this case being squeezed. The two converse suppositions of low and high inflexible rewards do not, however, lead to similarly opposed results. If profits are high there is a tendency towards expansion of output, but this is ultimately limited by what is physically possible. The total output of a country cannot exceed the physical capacity of her productive resources. If profits are low on the other hand there is a persistent tendency towards contraction. The process of contraction does not meet with a physical obstacle analogous to that which opposes itself to a limitless expansion. As contraction proceeds, it may, if confined to one country, produce a new equilibrium. By restricting output a country tends to confine herself to the fields in which her comparative advantage is greatest. By limiting the scope of her activity, she raises her own efficiency per unit. Thus the sum total of all rewards cannot be high in relation to her efficiency in the output which she actually undertakes; but they may be high in relation to her efficiency in the broader sphere of what she could undertake, were rewards not so high. High rewards are secured at the cost of the partial unemployment of her productive resources.

[1] Cf. the analysis of the relation of cost of production to increment of receipts in the case of the quasi-monopolistic producer of goods in ch. III, pp. 56–57.

A country which relies chiefly on the production of B goods is in a rather worse position than one relying chiefly on A goods, when faced with the demand by factors for rewards in excess of what efficiency justifies. The A goods country raises, at the cost of unemployment, the average productive efficiency of factors in the various fields of employment by the operation of the law of increasing productive costs in the production of A goods.[1] But B goods are often not subject to this law over a wide range on the productive side. The restriction of output may not raise the average efficiency on the productive side in respect of *each* of these goods. If the production of the least profitable types is abandoned altogether, average efficiency may be somewhat higher in the remaining field than it was in the whole field before. But in the types some output of which is still undertaken, there will probably be no gain of efficiency in production, the adjustment, if any, being made through the abandonment of the less accessible markets. But as the foreign competitor approaches, the new frontier may soon become as hard to defend as the old one. The higher reward is being paid in part out of a capital asset—goodwill. As time passes, if there is no adjustment of productive efficiency to reward, or reward to productive efficiency, more and more goodwill may have to be sacrificed progressively, and, without any further widening of the gap between reward and efficiency, unemployment will grow.

To recapitulate, the sum total of all rewards must be proportional to the efficiency of a country in respect of the output which she undertakes. The sum total of inflexible

---

[1] This means the real costs *decrease* and productive efficiency increases when production is restricted.

rewards may be low in relation to that efficiency, but this will be precisely offset by high profits. The sum total of inflexible rewards may also be high in relation to that efficiency, if profits are correspondingly low ; this condition is unstable, however, as output will tend to contract. Finally, the sum total of all rewards may be high in relation to the efficiency of a country in respect of her potential output ; in this case there will be unemployment.

The foregoing analysis did not take account of the fact that not all output is marketed at world prices. That level of rewards may be regarded as neither high nor low in relation to her efficiency which enables a country to sell at a normal rate of profit, enough to give employment to all productive resources *other than* those engaged in C industries. C goods may be divided into two classes, consumable C goods (and services) and immovable capital goods. What determines the proportion of total resources devoted to providing consumable C goods (and services) may be stated fairly simply. Since the total income is equal to the sum of rewards to all factors, the proportion of resources devoted to the production of C consumables is equal to the proportion of total income expended upon them. (This statement has to be modified if part of income is derived from foreign investments or foreign gifts ; more will be said of this later.) The proportion of productive resources devoted to the output of fixed capital is, in equilibrium, determined by the rate of saving of the community and the technique of industry. At any given time there is therefore a definite proportion of total productive resources, which, if the system is in equilibrium, are devoted to C output. The level of rewards proper to a country may therefore be defined as that which enables such a quantity of goods to be marketed at world prices with a normal rate of profit, that, if the employment so given is added to employment given by C industries when in their normal relation to the A and B industries, the productive resources of the country are in reasonably full employment. If inflexible rewards are higher than this there will be unemployment, if lower, inflated profits.

There is much popular misconception regarding the detriment to this country that is due to the prevalence of low wage rates elsewhere. Since many countries are less efficient than this country, wages must necessarily be lower in them; the low wage is offset by low efficiency. Of course the low wage may also be due to the ability of the other factors to secure a larger share of the product; in this case the low wage is offset by high profits or rents. Low wages in foreign countries are decried on the ground that they give those countries an unfair competitive advantage; this attitude is highly confused. A foreign country's power as a competitor depends on the volume and nature of her production; the payment of low wages will not allow her to force production above the level determined by the numbers and skill of her people. She cannot sell more than she can produce. We are benefited if the foreign country can maintain production at a high level, unless she happens to specialize in the goods which we export.[1] In this one case we are injured by her prosperity and would gain if her output declined. To complain of her low wages means nothing unless it means that we should like her to put her wages so high as to restrict her output and create unemployment in her own land; and this is more than we can in fairness expect.

Low wages abroad may be condemned for keeping

[1] Cf. ch. II, p. 40.

the health and efficiency of workpeople there at a low level and so reducing the real wealth of the foreign country. In accordance with the second principle of Chapter II, anything which reduces the real wealth of the outer world is likely to reduce the gain accruing to this country from foreign trade. But this is not the score on which low wages abroad are usually decried. The level of wages in foreign countries has no relevance to the proper level of wages at home.

Changes in general world level of A and B prices are clearly relevant; but it is important to guard against the fallacy of using the low costs or prices elsewhere *of particular commodities* as evidence that wages at home are too high. Rewards to factors are proportional to the general level of a country's efficiency. It does not follow that there is any meaning in saying that rewards in any particular trade are or should be proportional to the country's efficiency in that trade. Efficiency, i.e. the value of output per unit of factor employed in the production of a particular commodity, depends on how much output of the commodity is undertaken by the country. To make rewards proportional to the efficiency of factors producing a particular commodity in a country, when engaged in satisfying all and no more than that country's own needs for this commodity, would be equivalent to dispensing with all foreign trade. If it is said that rewards to factors producing a commodity are or should be proportional to their efficiency in producing that amount of the commodity which the country actually produces, the proposition is true but states nothing. For how much will she produce? That amount which, given the rewards to factors *and* their efficiency, she can market at home or abroad. Of the three variables, efficiency, rate of reward, and the amount of production of the particular commodity, if two are known the other can be determined. But if only one is known, efficiency, the other two cannot be deduced from that.

§ 6. *Summary*. The conclusions of this chapter may be summarized :

(i) For A goods there are common world prices. The price of each A commodity in one place will not differ from its price in another by more than the cost of transporting it between them, plus the monetary equivalent of any impediment to trade, such as a tariff, dividing them.

(ii) The prices of B goods also tend towards a common level. But the forces operating to bring about this result have to overcome greater friction than in the case of A goods ; moreover B goods of the same description produced in different centres are apt to differ to some extent in kind.

(iii) There is no world price level for C goods. The national price levels are only related through the relation of each to the price levels of the other classes. There are conditions in which national price levels for C goods will be equal, but these are not likely to be realized. Consumable C goods and all retail goods are likely to be more expensive in more efficient countries.

(iv) There is no world price for factors of production. Each national price level is proportional to the efficiency of the factors in making A and B commodities. A distinction must be drawn between the more and less easily adjustable prices of factors. If rigid rewards to factors are high in relation to the efficiency of the country, equilibrium is secured by unemployment in that country being more intense than elsewhere.

CHAPTER V

FOREIGN EXCHANGE

§ 1. *The Balance of Payments (introductory)*. If an imaginary boundary line were drawn around any area of the world's surface, an inventory could be made of all the payments moving over the line, some proceeding outwards, others inwards. These payments could be divided into those arising out of purchases, loans and gifts. Money may be paid in exchange for goods and services, it may be lent or repaid, or it may be given. This seems to be an exhaustive classification of the reasons for which money may pass from the pockets of residents on one side of the line to those of residents on the other side. It is not, however, quite all the money that passes over, for residents themselves may move out or in, taking money with them.

Payments out may thus be classified according to the purposes for which they are made as follows :

(i) Importation of goods and services.

(ii) (*a*) Loans to the outer world.
    (*b*) Repayment of loans previously made by the outer world to the area.

(iii) Gifts, including indemnity payments, made to the outer world.

(iv) (a) Expenditure of tourists travelling in the outer
world.

(b) Money taken by emigrants leaving the area for
the outer world.

The first of these (i) may be further subdivided :

(a) " Visible " import of commodities.

(b) Freight payments by firms in the area for the use of
foreign ships.

(c) Payments made for the use of such foreign services
as insurance, brokerage, etc.

(d) Interest and profit on foreign capital invested in
the area.

Payments coming into the area may be classified in a
similar way. Thus each division and subdivision involves
or may involve both payments out and in. It is important
to bear in mind on which side of the balance-sheet each
item comes. The importation of goods, the income
derived from investments made by foreigners in the
country, loans to foreigners and the expenditure of
nationals travelling abroad, for instance, all come on the
same side. The exportation of goods, the income from
foreign investments, foreign loans to the area, the expenditure of foreign tourists in the area all come on the other side.

Payments are often divided into those arising from
" visible " and those from " invisible " items. The
former class includes only the division (i) (a) above. All
other items are invisible.

The most elaborate statistical estimate of a balance of
payments is that undertaken by the United States Department of Commerce.[1] A large variety of " invisible "

[1] The Balance of International Payments of the United
States, annually since 1922.

sources of international payments have been sedulously explored. Estimates are made for such items as motion picture royalties, charitable contributions, telephone services, and underwriters' commissions, and payments arising from unconstitutional kinds of trade have not been left out of account.

Payments in and payments out may be cancelled against each other and the difference is the net balance of payments. If the payments in exceed the payments out the balance is called positive, active or favourable. If the imaginary boundary line happens to be a national frontier, the money in use within will probably not have currency outside and the payment will have to be mediated by a " foreign exchange " transaction, by which one national money is converted into another. These transactions can, however, only cover the payments which may be cancelled against each other ; the net balance, active or passive, cannot be met in this way ; local money can only be exchanged against foreign money in so far as there is a counterbalancing offer of foreign money to meet the offer of local money. If there is an unfavourable balance the excess of local money offered may be met by the offer of foreign money on short loan. But if we include short loans in estimating the balance and there remains a net deficit there is no means of covering it by a foreign exchange operation. If a gold, or silver, standard prevails within and without, gold, or silver, may be exported or imported to cover the net balance. From this it may be deduced that when all items as well as short loans are included in computing the balance, the net excess or deficit must be equal to the quantity of the standard metal imported or exported. If trade in the precious metals be included in computing the balance, there can be no excess or deficit. Payments out must be exactly equal to payments in. If the country is not on a gold (or silver) standard foreign trade in these metals should be reckoned along with that in other commodities, and, as in the other case, there must be an exact balance of payments in and out. This is a principle of cardinal importance in the subject and failure to appreciate it leads to much confusion of thought in popular discussion.

Official figures giving the visible trade in commodities usually show an active or passive balance. When " invisible " items, such as freight payments, merchants' profits, the payments made for the services of banking or insurance houses and interest on capital are brought in there may still be an active or passive balance. The state of this " balance on current account " has a considerable importance and interest of its own. But when long and short loans are also brought in, and movements of the precious metals, the balance can no longer be active or passive. It must be an exact balance and that not only in the long run, but from day to day and from moment to moment. Within any period, however short, all the British pounds sterling given in exchange for other currencies must be exactly equal to the pounds' worth of other currencies given in exchange for pounds sterling ; nor is there any other way of making payment except by the exportation of precious metals ; actual sterling may be remitted abroad by way of payment, but in that case the recipient must convert the sterling into his own currency if the payment is to be made negotiable in his country ; of course he may hold on to the pounds sterling and defer converting them : the holding of British currency abroad in this way is reckoned as a short loan to Great Britain.

§ 2. *The Gold Standard and Gold Points.* In the Foreign Exchange market those who, having the currency of one country, desire to acquire that of another, meet those who having the currency of the other desire to acquire that of the one. Foreign payments arising under whatever head are normally made through this market. A gold standard implies that the value of the currency is fixed in terms of gold. Reference to the official gold value of a unit of currency, a pound, a dollar, a franc, etc., determines the par of exchange. When the exchange is at par, a unit of one currency exchanges for units of another equal to the same amount of gold at the official valuations. For a gold standard to be effective the central monetary authority, the Central Bank or Treasury, must be willing to give in exchange for units of currency the amount of gold prescribed in the official valuation. Thus the holder of a currency in a country on an effective gold standard has always two possible methods of making a foreign payment : he may purchase the foreign currency in the foreign exchange market or he may acquire gold in exchange for currency from the central authority and remit it. The rate of exchange quoted in the market depends on the balance of supply and demand. If the demand for foreign currency is strong its value expressed in the market quotation tends to rise ; if the demand for the home currency is strong the value of the home currency tends to rise.

The language of the foreign exchange market is rather confusing. If the conventional method of quoting a rate of exchange is the number of units of foreign currency which may be obtained for a unit of the home currency (as in the British market so many dollars, francs, etc., to the pound), the rate for these currencies is said to rise, if a greater number can be obtained for one pound, that is, if the exchange value of the foreign currency falls. If on the other hand the conventional method of quoting is the number of pounds shillings and pence required to obtain a foreign unit (e.g. so many pence to the rupee), a rise in the rate means the same as a rise in the value of the currency quoted. To avoid confusion, the rise of a currency is always used, in what follows, to mean a rise in its value, irrespective of the conventional method of quotation.

The alternative means of making payment, the remission of gold, sets a limit to the fluctuation of foreign exchange rates. By the remission of gold the currency of a foreign gold standard country may always be obtained at par. But the remission of gold has a cost, the principal elements in which are the cost of transport, insurance and interest during the period of transit. If a would-be purchaser of foreign currency is to use the foreign exchange method, he must be able to get it at a cost at least equal to its par value plus the cost of remitting gold ; otherwise he will use the other method and remit gold. The quotation which makes the foreign exchange method equal in cost to the gold export method is called the gold export point and is the highest point to which the foreign exchange quotation of the foreign currency can rise while the gold standard is in operation in both countries. The quotation which makes the cost of the foreign exchange method for the foreigner to acquire the home currency equal to the cost of sending gold to the home country is called the gold import point and is the highest point to which the foreign exchange quotation of the home currency can rise.

It is not to be expected that the spontaneous flow of payments in and out arising out of normal transactions will balance day by day. On days when there is a strong spontaneous outward flow, foreign currency will become more expensive. This is a balancing factor. Banks and other firms which normally have balances in more than one centre can make the payments they need to make in any centre on a particular day out of the available balance in that centre, which is allowed to run down. They can thus, within limits, choose the time at which they convert one currency into another. The rise in the quotation of the foreign currency will lead them to postpone purchase if a relapse is expected at a later date. Foreign firms may also take advantage of the low price of the home currency to purchase it in advance of need. Thus if the spontaneous streams of payment are unequal, the movement in the quotation will thin one and supplement the other, tending to make them equal.[1] Speculation may also be a balancing element. If the fall in a quotation induces the expectation of a subsequent rise, the cheap currency will be brought to be resold at a profit at a later date. If the spontaneous flow of the demand for the home currency is sufficiently weak, its quotation may fall to the gold export point. The Central Bank must provide the gold or foreign exchange required to cover the deficiency, in exchange for units of currency, out of its reserve. Its reserve of foreign exchange may consist of deposits in foreign banks, actual foreign currency, or bills drawn on foreign firms.

Those desiring to purchase foreign currency will be equally well satisfied if the Bank provides them with gold or with foreign exchange in exchange for their own currency at a rate not higher than the gold export point.

[1] For the operation of the flow of bills of exchange as a balancing element, see below, pp. 90–92.

G

The gold standard will be maintained if, as soon as the exchange quotation reaches the gold export point, the Bank sells a sufficient quantity of gold or foreign exchange, to prevent its quotation rising above that point. To be able to do this the Bank must hold reserves of gold and/or foreign exchange.

If the Bank is legally obliged to offer gold in exchange for currency at par, the country is said to be on a gold standard. If it is only obliged to offer the currency of or bills on a foreign gold standard country at the gold export point, the country is said to be on a Gold Exchange standard. Even if the Bank is legally obliged to offer gold it may in fact offer foreign exchange. Provided that the would-be purchaser can get foreign currency from the central bank at a rate not higher than the gold export point, its quotation in the open market cannot rise above the gold export point. Individuals are concerned to get what they want at a rate not higher than this; it is indifferent to them whether they get gold at par or foreign exchange at the gold export point.

The central bank of a gold country is usually obliged by law to keep a certain reserve of gold. But it may keep the reserves, which it actually intends to use to meet a foreign exchange demand, in the form of foreign exchange. The Reichsbank is allowed to keep 25 per cent of the gold reserve required by law in the form not of gold but of foreign exchange. Many central banks keep part of the reserves they hold in excess of legal requirements in this form.

In order that the gold import point may also be effective, the central monetary authority, now usually the Central Bank, has the more welcome obligation to issue domestic currency in exchange for gold. This, however, is not always done at par. When the currency takes the form of gold coins the appropriate central authority to issue them is the Mint, which may wish to make a charge for coinage. Between 1666 and 1914 the English Mint made no such charge; it was, however, unwilling to issue coin on demand, but only after a period allowing time for the process of minting. The Bank of England was willing to issue coins on demand in return for a payment equivalent to interest on the process period, which was ultimately reduced to 1½d. on £3 17s. 10½d. (= 1 oz. 22 carat gold). This is the origin of the difference between the Bank's buying price and selling price of gold (£3 17s. 9d. and £3 17s. 10½d.) in the period 1925 to 1931, as laid down by the Act restoring the gold standard in 1925. Thus the difference between the gold export and import points was not equal to twice the cost of remitting the gold between London and the foreign centre, but twice that cost plus 1½d. an oz.

By widening the margin between its buying and selling price the Bank could widen the margin between the gold points. In his *Treatise on Money*[1] Mr. Keynes gave reasons for thinking as large a margin as 2 per cent desirable. Such an arrangement would not be inconsistent with a gold standard. The natural course of events on the other hand is tending to reduce the margin between gold points due to the cost of remission.[2]

When Hungary stabilized her currency in 1924 she explicitly adopted a Sterling Exchange standard. The value of her currency, the pengo, was fixed not in gold, but in sterling which was not itself at that time a gold standard currency. To maintain the position her central

[1] Op. cit., Vol. II, p. 325.
[2] Einzig, *International Gold Standard Movements*, ch. 9.

bank had to keep a reserve of sterling currency or sterling bills. The sterling exchange quotation was only allowed to fluctuate within limits analogous to the gold points. So any country might undertake to keep its currency stable in terms of some other currency. An objective standard, such as gold, is not a necessary condition of foreign exchange stability.

If the central bank is not obliged and does not in fact undertake[1] to buy and sell gold or foreign exchange in exchange for the local currency at fixed rates, there is no limit to possible fluctuations of foreign exchange rates in the open market. The rates may then move freely under the influence of supply and demand. The probable course of foreign exchange in these circumstances must be studied in relation to the influences affecting supply and demand.

§ 3. *Bills of Exchange.* Reference has been made to foreign bills of exchange. In the nineteenth century these were the principal means by which foreign payments were effected. An Englishman wishing to make a payment in Paris would authorize the French firm to draw a bill on him, while a Frenchman wishing to make a payment in London would purchase such a bill. The bills might be payable on sight or after the lapse of ninety days. The quotations of the foreign exchange markets referred to the rates at which such bills could be bought and sold. The use of the telegraph and cable has

[1] The Secretary of State for India and the Government of India did between them in fact undertake to buy and sell sterling exchange for rupees at fixed rates between 1900 and 1914, though not legally obliged to do so. India was thus effectively on a Gold Exchange standard in that period. India is now on a Sterling Exchange standard.

facilitated the more direct bartering of bank deposits in different countries against each other by means of a telegraphic transfer (" T.T."), and the quotation for a bill is now calculated from the T.T. quotation and the current rate of interest on the centre on which the bill is drawn; in the case of the South American exchanges, however, the bill rate remains the governing rate.

If someone in London has to make a payment in New York he may authorize the payee to draw a bill on him expressed in sterling payable at sight or with ninety days to run. The authorization is confirmed by his bank or accepting house, acting through its agent in New York. The drawer of the bill may sell it at once to his banker in New York for dollars. The present dollar value of a ninety day bill is computed by subtracting interest for ninety days at the market rate current in London, which gives its present sterling value, and translating that into dollars at the current rate of exchange. The New York banker may then remit it to London to have it accepted by the bank or accepting house, referred to above, on behalf of the drawee. When this has been done, the bill is a liability both of the drawer and the firm which accepts it. It may then be discounted in London, and the American banker can buy dollars with the proceeds by cable. The discount house or bank which discounts the bill in London is paid off by the acceptor when the bill matures. The creditor (drawer) thus receives his money approximately ninety days before the debtor (drawee) has to pay.

The drawer's banker may not choose to discount the bill in the London market at once ; he may instruct his London correspondent to hold it on his account. Whether he discounts it in London or has it held on his account depends upon the current rate of exchange and the comparative rates of interest in London and New York. The moment when the bill is discounted in London and the proceeds exchanged for dollars is really the moment at which the English community pays its debt to U.S.A. If sterling is low the American banker may defer discounting in the hopes of a rise. He will be still more influenced by current rates of interest. It will be remembered that the American banker paid the drawer for his bill a sum calculated from the current market rate in London. The American banker has purchased a short term investment yielding interest at the London rate. If the London rate is higher than the rate which he could get with his funds in New York, it is a good investment and he is tempted to hold it until it matures If the rate falls in London the present value of the bill rises and he is tempted to part with it. If the rate rises in London after he has acquired it, the present value of the bill falls and the American banker is subjected to a loss, unless he holds it till its maturity.

Thus a low sterling quotation and, more important, a high relative rate of interest in London will check the discount of sterling bills in London, and thus reduce the offer of sterling in the foreign exchange market and so have a restorative effect on a passive balance of payments. It should be noted that the volume of sterling bills held on foreign account in London or abroad constitutes along with foreign deposits in the country the national sight liability to foreigners.

A speculator in foreign exchange may lend his support to a weak currency by drawing a bill on his own agent in the strong centre. The bill is discounted at once and its proceeds used to purchase the cheap currency in the hope that it may be possible to buy back the expensive currency at a cheaper rate before the bill has matured. The margin of profit for such transactions is, however, very narrow.

§ 4. *Forward Foreign Exchange.* Something must also be said of forward dealing. If a currency becomes cheap, those who have payments to make in the future may desire to take advantage of the present rate without actually spending the money required to make the payment in advance ; they may desire to secure themselves against future fluctuation, which is, of course, highly important in the case of payments to and from a country not on a stable standard. The purchase of forward foreign currency consists of a promise to pay home currency for it at a specified future date at a rate agreed on now. The rate agreed on may differ from the rate at which foreign currency can be purchased now (the " spot " rate). What determines the difference ? Dealers in forward exchange have to satisfy the demands of their clients ; they undertake to deliver the foreign currency at a specified future time at a rate to be fixed now ; they may be quite unwilling to speculate on the foreign currency becoming cheaper or not becoming dearer in the interval ; consequently they must cover themselves by purchasing the foreign money at once ; this they invariably do. In doing so they have transferred their liquid funds from one centre to another on the strength of a contract which enables them to bring those funds home again at the rate agreed on.

The advantage or disadvantage of having their funds for a time at the foreign centre depends on the rate of interest which they can earn there compared with the rate of interest which they can earn at home. If the rate is higher abroad, it is an advantage, for which they are prepared to pay by selling forward currency below the spot rate. The forward deal enables them to earn the higher rate abroad without running the risk of the exchange moving against them before they bring their funds back. The forward dealers therefore tend to be willing to sell forward currency at a discount compared with spot by an amount equal, after deducting a commission for themselves, to the excess of what they can earn in the short market of the foreign country over what they could earn in the short market of the home country during the period of contract. If the rate is lower abroad, the forward rate exceeds the spot rate by the excess of what they could have earned in the home market over what they can earn in the foreign market plus a commission for themselves.

Actually dealers are both buying and selling foreign currencies forward and their contracts made in the course of a day may cancel each other out. But every one must be covered when it is made, to avoid risk; if there is an equal balance at the end of the day the discount on forward sales cancels the premium on forward purchases (or vice versa) and the dealer's net profit is equal to the sum of the commissions on both.

If there is a lack of confidence in the future of a currency, those who wish to sell it forward will exceed those who wish to purchase it forward. The spot sales of forward dealers covering themselves will exceed spot purchases, and the opinion about the future of the currency is thus reflected in a present excess of supply over demand and a weakening in its spot quotation. This shadow, which the future casts before it, is particularly important in the case of currencies the exchange in which is not stabilized.

It is the difference between gold export and import points that allows short rates of interest to be at a different level in centres on the same standard.

If the rate in London is lower than the rate in New York, why should not an American who has English connections draw a bill on his agent in London, get it accepted and discounted there and acquire funds at the low rate for some purely domestic purpose ? If such operations could be carried out on a sufficiently large scale the English rate would be forced up to the American level. But they cannot be. For the spot sterling quotation may rise in the interval and, when the American comes to acquire sterling to honour his bill, he may have to pay a larger number of dollars per pound than he acquired at the outset when he discounted the bill in London and sold the proceeds for dollars. If the maximum possible fluctuation is ·5 per cent, which represents a loss on a ninety-day bill of 2 per cent per annum, the rate in London would have to be more than 2 per cent lower than in New York to cover the risk of such a fluctuation. May not the American safeguard himself by purchasing forward sterling at the outset, that is, at the same moment that he sells spot sterling ? No, because if the London rate of discount is below the American rate the forward price of sterling will exceed the spot price by precisely the amount which the American hopes to gain by borrowing money at the cheaper centre. The larger the gap between the gold points, the greater the possible divergence of interest rates between two centres with close commercial connections. When the difference between rates is larger than that which the margin between gold points ought to allow, that must either be due to a lack of confidence in the stability of the currency in the high rate centre or because the firms in the high rate centre have not sufficient connections with accepting and discount houses in the low rate centre to enable them to borrow there on a sufficiently large scale to produce an equalizing effect on the rates.

§ 5. *The Monetary System.* In a modern community money consists chiefly of bank deposits. For smaller payments currency (notes and coins) is also used. Of this currency a considerable proportion often consists of bank notes. Bank deposits and bank notes may be jointly designated by the expression, bank money.

An individual can acquire bank money in one of three ways :

(i) If the country is on the gold standard he may pay in gold to the central bank (or another bank) and acquire a deposit or bank notes in exchange. Similarly when gold is taken out of or sold by the banks, bank money is withdrawn from circulation. Consequently the aggregated gold holdings of the banks show roughly the net outstanding quantity of bank money created in this way.

(ii) He may pay a cheque drawn on another account in to his own and so acquire a deposit. Such a transaction merely represents the transfer of a deposit from one individual to another and does not involve a net increase of deposits. He may pay in a cheque and draw out notes, but this merely represents the conversion of one kind of bank money (a deposit) into another (notes), and does not involve a net increase of bank money in the country. Similarly, an individual may pay in notes and acquire a deposit.

(iii) He may obtain a loan from the bank, which he

draws out, or allows to stand as a deposit in his name, or, more probably, pays over to someone else. This represents the creation of new bank money. Bank loans thus create deposits and/or put bank notes into circulation. The repayment of a loan cancels a deposit and/or withdraws bank notes from circulation.

Banks make loans to individuals at call or short notice, by the discount of bills with a stated time to run, and against the deposit of collateral security. Banks also make loans, like private individuals, by the purchase of investments. An individual can acquire bank money by selling securities to a bank. The purchase of securities by a bank creates new bank money and the sale of securities by a bank destroys it.

The aggregate amount of outstanding bank loans, including their investments in securities, shows roughly the net outstanding quantity of bank money created in this way.

Thus the total amount of bank money is roughly equal to the gold holdings of the banks plus their outstanding loans. (The equation would be exact but for the fact that banks, like other concerns, charge a price for their services, have running expenses and distribute dividends. It is assumed in what follows that these kinds of payment in and out balance exactly.)

The circulating medium of the community, apart from small token coins, consists of bank money, possibly gold, and the Government note issue, if any. The amount of outstanding bank money is equal, it has been shown, to the amount of outstanding bank loans plus the net amount of gold paid into the banks. Thus, in the absence of a Government issue, the total outstanding medium of the country is equal to the total of outstanding bank loans plus the monetary gold in the country. The latter of these quantities is equal to the aggregated net active balance of payments of the country in past years, less the quantity of gold absorbed by the industrial arts.

In the remote past the quantity of monetary gold (or silver) in the country formed a large proportion of the total quantity of money. The balance of foreign payments had consequently an important direct influence on this quantity. In more recent times bank money, created by bank loans, has contributed by far the greater part of the total. In the U.S.A., for instance, which has been held to be carrying an unduly large amount of monetary gold in recent years, monetary gold stood at 4·59 billion dollars, and bank money at 57·93 billion dollars at the end of 1930.[1] The United Kingdom held £148 million of monetary gold at the same time and £2668 million of bank money.[2] The position of France was even then exceptional; she held 54 billion francs of gold and only 126 billion francs of bank money.[3]

The balance of payments has been supposed, however, to have had an important indirect influence on the quantity of money in circulation in more recent times. The banking system as a whole used in pre-war days, it has been said, to regulate the total quantity of money, so as to bear a constant or nearly constant ratio to the monetary gold in the country. This regulation is presumably what is meant by the expression, " pre-war rules of the game," when used with reference to the gold standard. These rules were the theme of economists for more than half a century, but whether they were

[1] F.R.B. Annual Report for 1931.
[2] *Statistical Year Book of the League of Nations*, 1931–2.
[3] *Ibid.*

commonly put into operation is open to serious doubt. Now that economists have largely lost interest in them, they have become dear to the heart of financial experts (outside France and America). An invention of academic writers, practical men implicitly believe that they once formed part of the mechanism of the real world, and that their observance would be a panacea for present monetary ills.

The quantity of money is almost entirely determined by the quantity of loans made by the banking system ; and that, in its turn, in countries with a fully developed banking system, is entirely determined by the policy of the central bank.

§ 6. *The Central Bank and the Balance of Payments.* If a country is on a gold standard and there is a passive balance of foreign payments, it is the duty of the central bank to make good the deficiency by being willing to convert domestic money into gold at par or into foreign exchange at the gold export point. Law usually prescribes that the central bank shall keep a certain reserve of gold against its note issue ; some countries, of which the United States is one, also have a legal reserve against deposit liabilities. If the law lays down that a certain percentage of liabilities (of either form) must be backed by gold, only the gold held in excess of the required percentage is actually available. The laws of the United States and Germany, however, allow the reserve to fall below the required percentage for short periods on payment of a progressive tax. In England there is only a legal requirement in respect of notes, and it takes the form that all notes issued in excess of a certain quantity must have a 100 per cent backing.

When there is an adverse balance it is more usual for the bank to be called upon to give gold to meet its deposit liabilities than to meet its notes in circulation ; the volume of notes in circulation satisfies the requirements of the community for small change and these are not likely to be reduced immediately in consequence of a passive balance. It follows that the gold backing of the notes is not legally available to meet the demands upon the bank reserve in the form in which they usually come. The "free" gold is what the bank has in addition to the legal requirement. The Bank of England usually issues notes against all the gold it has and retains the excess of notes issued over notes paid out in the Banking Department ; the notes in the Banking Department thus represent the "free" gold reserve of the bank. This alone is available to meet an adverse balance. By the Act of 1928 the bank was allowed, after consultation with the Treasury, to issue notes for a limited period in addition to the £260 million normally allowed. This really means that the bank would in a crisis be allowed to tap part of the gold behind the notes. In the crisis of August 1931, £15 million of the gold was released in this way. A more drastic measure of release is to suspend the Bank Act and thus make all the gold behind the notes available. This expedient was regularly adopted in the crises of the nineteenth century. It was not, however, adopted before the suspension of gold payments on September 21, 1931 ; the bank preferred to meet the drain by raising foreign credits of an amount approximately equal to its tied gold (£130 million).

In the gold standard period of 1925–31 the notes in the Banking Department (=the "free" gold) fluctuated between approximately £60 million and £25 million.

This was a very small sum either by comparison with the total outward payments of the country of the order of £1200 million per annum, or with the total amount of money in the hands of the public of the order of £2600 million.

When the gold standard is in operation it is thus necessary for the bank, if it is to fulfil its obligations, to secure that foreign payments, not counting in gold bullion movements, do approximately balance, or, at least, are not excessively unfavourable.

The immediate weapon which the bank has to hand is to raise its rate of discount. This can be made effective in the market by the sale of securities, which the bank can undertake on its own initiative, and which reduces the volume of its outstanding loans and so makes borrowable money scarce. In normal times the immediate effect of the raising of the bank rate is to make the balance of payments more favourable, for reasons already explained. The country becomes a less advantageous centre to borrow in than before and a more favourable centre to hold deposits in; this fact decreases short loans by the country and increases short loans to the country.

If, however, there is any suspicion owing to abnormal circumstances that this weapon will not be effective in equating the foreign balance, it becomes ineffective. The difference between the rates of interest in different centres is small compared with the risk of loss, if the gold standard is suspended. Thus, if it is feared that the gold standard may be suspended, the high rate ceases to attract short loans to the country, and fails to make the foreign payments balance. And thus, if the foreign drain persists, the gold standard has to be suspended.

Suspicion, when it arises, is itself the cause of an extended drain, for those who hold liquid balances hasten to exchange them for a currency that is not suspect. A monetary system is seldom strong enough to withstand a loss of confidence.

The weapon of a high bank rate, which the central bank has to hand, has been considered so far from the short period point of view only. If it is possible for fundamental forces to be at work making for a sustained adverse balance of payments, the attraction of foreign deposits and the repulsion of short term foreign borrowers through a high rate of interest clearly will not by itself bring the balance into permanent equilibrium. It is necessary, therefore, to examine the fundamental conditions that determine the sizes of the inflowing and outflowing streams of payment.

§ 7. *Foreign Exchange in the Absence of a Gold Standard.* If the country is not on the gold standard, the Foreign Exchange method is the only method of making a foreign payment, and the rates move freely under the influence of supply and demand. Like other prices, they must make supply equal to demand. It does not follow that the supply and demand arising out of payments due in respect of normal transactions must balance from day to day, for when there is no par of exchange, speculative operations play an especially important part. Since changes in the rates may be large, successful speculation can yield a high rate of profit. Under the influence of speculative dealing, the rate of exchange may be steadied at a level which in the view of the speculators will equate the prospective non-speculative supply and demand. If, however, there is complete uncertainty as to the future, speculation may induce violent fluctuations. If the currency is moving in a certain direction, e.g. downwards, speculators will anticipate the future, and the present rate will tend to stand not at a point that balances present non-speculative supply and demand, but at one which is expected to balance non-speculative supply and demand three months, six months or a year hence. This process was amply illustrated in the external "undervaluation" of the inflating currencies after the war. Relatively to existing non-speculative supply and demand, their price in terms of stable currencies was permanently too low; but in relation to what was destined to happen in the ensuing year, the present undervaluation was often moderate.

In the next chapter the fundamental circumstances determining the volume of non-speculative payments in and out will be examined.

H

CHAPTER VI

THE BALANCE OF TRADE

§ 1. *Equilibrium in Simplified Conditions.* The equilibrium of foreign payments can best be approached in stages. In the first stage it is well to suppose that all payments are in respect of goods and services traded. Since it is dangerous to consider foreign transactions in isolation and their interconnection with national production and consumption must always be borne in mind, it will be supposed in this stage that not only is there no foreign investment, but no domestic investment either. Individuals and corporate bodies in their capacity of final consumers spend the whole of their incomes. There is no addition to the capital goods of the country.

Consumers' expenditure is divided between A and B goods and C goods.[1] Income is wholly derived from the sale of these goods. Two fundamental propositions apply to the whole of this analysis and not to the first stage of it only. First, the amount of income derived from the sale of C consumable goods is equal to the amount of income devoted to the purchase of them. Since C goods are by definition not capable of entering into international trade, their purchase always involves payment by certain members of the community to other members of the community. The sum total of money paid in respect of them is necessarily equal to the sum

[1] For definitions of these, see pp. 59–62.

total of money received through the sale of them.
Secondly, the excess (or deficiency) of the sale of
A and B goods over the purchase of them must be equal
to the active (or passive) balance of trade. For the
amount of income derived from the sale of A and B goods
by nationals to nationals must be equal to the amount of
income spent on the purchase of A and B goods by
nationals from nationals. The excess of the output of A
and B goods over the purchase of them and the active
balance of trade[1] are used in what follows as interchangeable terms.

In the conditions of the first stage of this analysis the
amount of income derived from all the sales of A and B
goods is equal to the amount of income expended upon
them and trade balances. For, since all income received
is also spent, and the sums received in respect of C goods
are equal to those spent upon them, the residue on each
side of the equation, namely, the sums received in respect
of A and B goods and those spent upon them must be
equal to each other.

This state of simplified equilibrium repays examination. The amount of A and B output which a country
will undertake depends on (i) the world price level, (ii)
the rewards of factors of production at home, (iii) the
efficiency of those factors and (iv) the course of events in
the preceding period ; (ii) and (iii) may be compounded
into the expression, efficiency-rewards to factors of
production ; (iv) may be explained as follows.   In
Chapter IV a distinction was drawn between the relatively
inflexible rewards to factors and the residual item of
profits.[2] If a force begins to operate which would tend

---

[1] In the arguments of this chapter, trade is taken to include
the purchase and sale of current services.   [2] Cf. p. 74.

ultimately to reduce A and B output, viz. a fall in the
world price level or a rise in efficiency rewards, output
may at first be maintained at its pre-existent level by the
squeezing of profits. As time goes on, the profit earning
factor will reassert itself; plant will not be renewed or
extended, and output will sag. Consequently if at any
point of time the values of the terms in (i), (ii) and (iii)
are known, it cannot be deduced what the level of output
will be without some reference to preceding history.
Profits may be in process of reasserting themselves or
they may be inflated, and a change in the level of output
may go forward without any further change in world
prices or efficiency-rewards. It is possible to rewrite
the determining factors set out above as follows : (i) the
world price level, (ii) the efficiency-rewards of factors,
and (iii) the state of profits. If these are known, the
volume of A and B output may be deduced. For all output will be undertaken, of which the price covers the
cost including a normal profit.

The proportion of expenditure that is devoted to A
and B purchases depends on (i) the tastes of consumers
and (ii) the relation of the world price level to the C goods
price level. The proportion of income derived from A
and B sales is equal to the proportion of income devoted
to their purchase. Consequently if I_t stands for the
income derived from the sale of A and B goods, h for the
proportion of expenditure devoted to them and I for
total income :

$$I = \frac{1}{h}(I_t)$$

Thus the total income of the community will be larger,
the more favourable the determining conditions are to a
large income derived from the sale of A and B goods and

the smaller the proportion of income devoted to the purchase of them.   Up to the stage of reasonably full employment A and B output will expand the higher are world prices and the lower efficiency-rewards ; beyond that stage a rise of prices or a fall of efficiency-rewards would merely lead to the progressive inflation of profits.

Next it is desirable to examine what happens if there is some disturbance in the fundamental conditions.   Suppose that, other things remaining the same, there is an improvement in productive efficiency in some other country in respect of goods which we export, e.g. in the Japanese cotton piece-goods industry, and a consequent shrinkage in a foreign market.   This involves some loss of advantage which England was formerly able to derive from her foreign trade and a deterioration in her position. Two kinds of adjustment are possible : (i) the rewards to factors may be adjusted so as to keep productive resources in reasonably full employment ;   (ii) factors may be allowed to go out of employment.

(i) The situation may be met by a reduction of rewards (of profits only, perhaps, in the first instance, and subsequently of inflexible rewards), so as to sustain employment in the A and B industries at its old level.   Employment in these industries being the same and rewards lower, income earned in them will be somewhat lower and this will cause repercussions in the C industries ; these repercussions will be similar to but smaller than those which would occur on the alternative hypothesis of unemployment being allowed to occur in the A and B industries and will be discussed under that head.   (Inflexible rewards in the A and B industries might indeed, on reasonable assumptions as to the elasticity of demand for

English A and B output, be reduced so drastically that incomes in these industries were sustained at their old level and output increased. This could only occur if there was initially some slack of unemployed to be taken up and is an unlikely eventuality.)

The reduction of rewards might be concentrated in the cotton piece-goods industry or diffused generally. In the former case cotton operatives and other cotton factors would carry the whole detriment, due to the worsening of the position, by reducing their standard of living. There would be an infringement of the second principle laid down in Chapter III[1] for maximizing the gain by trade, namely, that rewards for equal effort should be equal in different occupations. The notion that each industry should pay the wages (and other rewards) that it can bear, though often recommended as being " dictated by the laws of supply and demand," is the opposite of the true economic principle.[2] Rewards should be made to approximate to equality in all occupations. Rewards in the country as a whole, however, can only be pushed above what the capacity of the country can bear, at the cost of unemployment.

If, on the other hand, there is a general reduction of rewards in all occupations, A and B output as a whole may be sustained, the reduction in cotton output being made good by an increase in other fields. The burden of the deterioration will be widely diffused through a general decline in the standard of living all round. If the adverse turn in the situation consists in nothing more than the loss of a particular market, the reduction required may

[1] Cf. p. 44, (i).
[2] For some concession to the opposite principle, however, see ch. III, p. 51.

well be small ; some retardation in the normal rate of
advance may be sufficient. But if many adverse factors
are at work simultaneously, the burden to be borne may
be more serious.

If the country is on a gold standard or, in the absence
of a gold standard, is committed to the policy of maintaining her rates of exchange with all or most other
countries stable, the reduction in rewards must take
the form of an outright money reduction. Otherwise, it
may be brought about through a depreciation in the
value of her currency in terms of other currencies.
The latter method of securing reduction can be carried
out with greater ease and equity as between different
interests ; it is discussed in a subsequent chapter.[1] In
this chapter a regime of stable exchanges will be
assumed.

In the modern world rewards to factors, other than
profits, tend to be fixed with some rigidity ; there is
much advantage in this rigidity, both as a safeguard
against sectional and general exploitation[2] and because
attempts to secure equilibrium through a reduction in
money rewards may set up a vicious circle of monetary
deflation and fail after all to achieve a reduction in real
rewards.[3]

(ii) If real rewards are not reduced, what will the nature
of the new equilibrium be? Full equilibrium in one sense
of the term will not be achieved, since there must be
some unemployment in the new situation.[4] But there

---

[1] Ch. VII.   [2] Cf. ch. IV, p. 74.

[3] These advantages, however, probably do not outweigh
the disadvantages, if an unreformed gold standard is postulated.

[4] If special devices for increasing employment, such as
employment subsidies, are excluded.

will be a new equilibrium in which receipts and expenditure, and exports and imports balance. In the new position A and B output and a fortiori A and B income will be reduced. It is necessary to examine the repercussions in the C industries.[1] Let us retain the supposition that individuals spend the whole of their incomes, neither adding to nor taking from their monetary holdings. In this case the loss of incomes in the A and B industries will be accompanied by a loss of incomes in the C industries sufficient to reduce the purchase of A and B goods by the amount that income from their sales has fallen off. Thus, provided that consumers do not spend more than they receive, purchasing power will be automatically reduced by a sufficient amount to entail a reduction in imports equal to that in exports.

This may be traced out. Suppose an initial loss of income in the A and B industries of $£p$. The individuals involved spend $£p$ less. This reduction is divided among the two main classes of expenditure. If expenditure on A and B goods is reduced by $£q_1$, that on C goods is reduced by $£p-q_1$. The income of the C industries is now reduced by $£p-q_1$ and individuals in these industries will spend less; if they spend $£q_2$ less on A and B goods, they will spend $£p-q_1-q_2$ less on C goods, and there will be a further consequential reduction of incomes in C industries of $£p-q_1-q_2$. This entails a further reduction of expenditure on both categories. Reduction of incomes in the C industries will proceed by the progressive transfer of reduction, until there is no more reduction to transfer. This

[1] It will be remembered that even if A and B output is sustained, there will be some though smaller repercussions of this kind, *vid. sup.* p. 107.

happens when $£p-(q_1+q_2+\ldots)$ is zero, i.e. when
$$q_1+q_2+\ldots=p.[1]$$

But the left-hand side of this equation is the sum of all the reductions in expenditure on A and B goods, while p is the initial loss of income from A and B sales. Thus the reduction in A and B purchases is equal to the reduction in A and B sales. This result that, provided no one spends more than he receives in income, total income will be reduced sufficiently to curtail expenditure on imports by the amount that exports have declined has absolute generality. Moreover, the whole process is simultaneous, so that the transition from one equilibrium to the other occurs without lapse of time. Far-reaching complications arise, when the simplifying suppositions of this enquiry do not hold. A clear understanding of this most simple and fundamental type of case is a necessary preliminary to the study of complications.

It is desirable also to trace the repercussions in the outer world. An improvement in productive efficiency has been registered in the Japanese cotton piece-goods industry. Three possibilities may be considered. (i) Rewards in this industry may be instantly raised, so that there is no fall in the price of these goods and no tendency for production to be transferred from England to Japan. In this case England will be completely preserved from feeling the effects of the change. There will be a residue of unemployed factors in the Japanese industry which will not be reabsorbed. (ii) Rewards in Japanese industry may be raised generally by an amount sufficient to preserve the general level of employment in Japan at its *status quo ante*. Cotton output will be increased and other

[1] The series on the left-hand side of this equation will be infinite, since q_r is always less than $p_r-(q_1+\ldots+q_{r-1})$.

output reduced ; (iii) Rewards in Japan may remain stationary, output and income in the cotton industry rising and diffusing new employment in Japanese C industries, until her total purchase of A and B goods has risen by the amount that her income from the sale of cotton goods rose. The third alternative is only possible if there was initially some slack of unemployment in Japan, which could be taken up. If at the outset the employment position was good, but none the less inflexible rewards were not raised, profits would become inflated, and *total* rewards would rise in Japan by the amount postulated under (ii).

In the new equilibrium of cases (ii) and (iii), Japan will purchase additional A and B goods from the world pool of a value equal to that of her increment of income in the cotton industry, just as England will reduce her purchase by an amount equal to her loss of income there. If the demand for cotton piece-goods is elastic in the world, the increment will be greater than the decrement, and there will be an improved market for A and B goods generally. To this extent the detriment to England will be mitigated, as she may be able to increase her other A and B output at the old level of rewards. On the other hand there is another circumstance tending to aggravate the detriment to England. Since the unity of the world market for B goods is imperfect, there will be some weakening in the price level of English B goods and a strengthening of the price level of Japanese B goods. A secondary deterioration due to this cause is likely to be more severe in a country which specializes in the production of B rather than of A goods.

Returning to the effects of the diffusion of unemployment in the home country, if h, the proportion of expenditure devoted to A and B purchases is the same in the new equilibrium as in the old, the proportionate reduction in output will be the same in the C as it is in the A and B industries. In the new state of affairs, the equilibrium equation,

$$I = \frac{I}{h}(I_t)$$

will hold. If h is the same as before, total income will have been reduced in the same proportion as income derived from A and B sales, and therefore income derived from C sales will also be reduced in that same proportion.

In the case where the adverse turn in the circumstances involves the fall in price of a commodity, some change in h is to be expected unless the elasticity of demand for it is equal to one. If the demand is elastic, a rise of h will occur, and the proportionate reduction in total income will be more than that in A and B income.[1] If the demand is inelastic the proportionate reduction in total income will be less.

An interesting variation on this theme may be mentioned. Suppose that workers thrown out of employment continue to be paid a smaller income from some source. The reduction of expenditure in the community is then equal to the reduction in the expenditure of the unemployed plus the reduction in the expenditure of those still in employment that is due to their having to provide funds for the unemployed. To compute h it is necessary to ascertain not the proportions in which a representative worker divides his expenditure, but the proportion in

[1] A rise in h occurring spontaneously will give rise to the same problems as the loss of a foreign market.

which the expenditure actually curtailed was divided. Since the necessaries of life, food, etc., are apt to belong to the A and B category, the actual reduction of expendituse on A and B goods is less than if the unemployed workers simply ceased to spend. The consequential diffusion of unemployment required to secure a balance of A and B sales and purchases is *pro tanto* greater.

Another type of case may be considered. Suppose that there is a general fall of prices in the outer world, due to monetary dislocation. The situation may be met in England by a proportionate reduction of rigid rewards. Otherwise there will be a fall in all or most lines of A and B output and a consequential diffusion of unemployment in the C industries. The effects would be analogous to those in the case already considered but correspondingly more severe. There is, however, a mitigating circumstance. There is probably some inelasticity in the demand for A and B goods considered as a category. The fall in the price of these will then cause a reduction in the proportion of income expended upon them. This means that the recession in the C industries will be less than the recession in the A and B industries. For instance, the equilibrium equation

$$I = \frac{1}{h}(I_t)$$

shows that if there is a reduction of A and B incomes of 10 per cent and at the same time a reduction in the proportion of income spent on A and B output of 5 per cent, the reduction in total income will only be $5\frac{5}{19}$ per cent.[1] This disproportion in the effect of a fall in world

[1] $$\frac{1}{\frac{95}{100}} \times \frac{90}{100} = \frac{94\frac{14}{19}}{100}$$

prices on the different categories of industry has been manifest in England in the last ten years, and everywhere in the last three, the international goods industries being more severely hit than the domestic industries.

§ 2. *Transition in Simplified Conditions.* In what has been said so far, it has been assumed that at every point consumers spend all and no more than all their income. On this assumption, the transitition from one equilibrium to another is instantaneous and presents no special problems. All that is necessary is to enquire into the nature of the old and the new equilibrium. The assumption is, however, an improbable one. Two circumstances likely to upset it must be sharply distinguished.

(i) When the new equilibrium is reached, the total income of the community stands at a lower level. It is reasonable therefore to expect that it will collectively be holding a smaller monetary balance. Consequently at some point in the transition there will have been either an excess of expenditure over income (involving a passive balance) equal to the reduction of monetary requirements, or a repayment of loans to the banks equal to the same amount, or some excess of expenditure and some repayment of loans, the sum of the two being equal to that amount. This is a necessary feature of the transition from one equilibrium to another and prevents the simultaneous adjustment postulated in the foregoing section.

(ii) It may happen that during the recession the excess of expenditure (=passive balance) would, if unchecked, be greater than the amount by which monetary requirements will ultimately be reduced. The scope and permanence of the change may not at first be realized ; firms and individuals may keep going by reducing their monetary balances below the level that will ultimately prove desirable. The diffusion of unemployment and contraction in the C industries may accordingly be delayed, imports meanwhile exceeding exports.

If the gold standard or any other form of stable foreign exchange regime is in operation, as is supposed in this chapter, the central bank has to cover any passive balance that is generated by parting with its reserves of gold or foreign exchange. These, however, are apt to be small by comparison either with the total amount of money in the country[1] or with the total volume of foreign payments. It may be impossible to meet the total passive balance generated during the transition. To safeguard its position it may (a) cause the adverse trade balance to be covered by attracting short term loans to the country by raising the market rate of discount, and/or (b) take up the slack money by the process of internal deflation (curtailment of loans). Capital movements are excluded from the picture at this stage of the argument. Let it suffice to say here that the attraction of short loans from abroad (a. sup.) is only a suitable remedy for a passive balance if that is destined to be subsequently offset by an active balance. Seasonal discrepancies in the balance are properly covered by this device. That part of the passive balance which is due to the second reason mentioned in the last paragraph may be rightly so covered. That part, however, which is due to a permanent reduction in monetary requirements will not be offset by an active balance at a subsequent date. This permanent reduction may be covered out of the reserves of the central bank ; if it is, the proportion

[1] Cf. pp. 98–101.

of reserves to liabilities of the central bank will be reduced
below its former level and may become dangerously low.
If the proportion is to be restored to its former level
some measure of internal deflation cannot be avoided.
This may have further repercussions, which must be
discussed when internal capital movements have been
introduced into the picture.

Great Britain's return to the gold standard in 1925,
involving a rise in the rate at which sterling exchanged
for foreign currency of about 10 per cent, entailed an
alteration in the relation between home efficiency rewards
and world prices of approximately that amount. If
efficiency rewards were not to be reduced in proportion,
there would necessarily be some measure of additional
unemployment in the new equilibrium position ; all
industry was to be expected to suffer but not in the same
degree as the export industries (cf. concluding sentence
of last section). In the transition there would be a
tendency towards a passive balance. This was met by
the normal method of making the foreign balance on
short loan account more favourable (*a. sup.*) and also by
the less usual method of discouraging long term foreign
lending. In its anxiety not to oppress British industry,
the Bank of England did not push the remedy of internal
deflation (*b. sup.*) to the point which the logic of the
situation required. The stabilization of sterling, which
made London a more suitable place for foreigners to hold
floating balances (=foreign deposits plus undiscounted
sterling bills held on foreign account[1]), gave much
fortuitous assistance to the Bank in its application of the
first remedy. The consequence was that our outstanding
sight liability to foreigners was not only increased during

[1] Cf. ch. V, p. 92.

the process of transition, but remained high when some sort of new equilibrium was achieved, and the amount of internal deflation which the Bank had to apply was less than it otherwise would have been.

British industry was thus spared a nasty dose of deflation ; but the gold standard was not re-established on a firm foundation. The reduction in home monetary requirements consequent upon its restoration was partly covered by inducing foreigners to hold more deposits in England than they had done before. Foreign deposits may be withdrawn in an emergency ; they should properly be regarded as a negative gold reserve. Thus the Bank really let the country's reserve available for meeting a passive balance in future run down to a negative figure. An attempt to restore it to a normal level would necessarily have involved severe internal deflation. The Bank may well have been justified in avoiding this injurious measure ; it was probably better not to fortify too strongly a gold standard hastily and injudiciously resumed. Its failure to cover the passive balance generated in 1931 was the natural consequence of the Bank's previous policy.

§ 3. *The Balance of all Payments on Current Account.* The equilibrium position when there are other items on current account in the foreign balance may next be considered. Such items are interest and profit on foreign investments, gifts, indemnity payments. If capital movements are still excluded, then in equilibrium a passive balance of trade is offset by an active balance on the other items and vice versa. A and B purchases are equal to the income from A and B sales plus the net active foreign balance on other items. The greater this net active balance the larger *ceteris paribus* will the total income of the community be. If F stands for the net active balance on other items, in equilibrium,

$$I = \frac{1}{h}(I_t + F).$$

Thus a rise of £100 p.a. in F will, *ceteris paribus*, not merely increase I by £100 p.a., but by $\frac{£100}{h}$ p.a. The receipt of £100 will be balanced in part by the expenditure of its recipients on A and B goods, in part by that of those consequentially given new employment in the C industries on A and B goods.

If a reduction in F occurs the opposite results follow. This may be illustrated by supposing that, on a condition in which foreign payments balance, there supervenes the necessity to make an indemnity payment. The people vote the required sum by taxation. Suppose that there is no change in world prices or rewards to factors at home and consequently no increase in A and B output. The people will have less money to spend by the amount of the tax they have voted. There will at once be some curtailment of the purchase of consumable A and B goods by the tax-payers and of A and B raw materials by those producing C consumable goods for the tax-payers. This primary reduction in A and B purchases will not be sufficient to cover the indemnity, for presumably only part of the income lost by the additional taxation would have gone to the purchase of A and B goods and materials. There will also be a reduction in the purchase of C goods. This will lead to a reduction in domestic employment and to a further curtailment of A and B purchases owing to the loss of purchasing power by those thrown out of work. The unemployment will be

I

extended progressively until the reduction of A and B purchases through loss of purchasing power is sufficient to cover the indemnity.

The unemployment is not, however, inevitable. It can be cured by the factors of production consenting to take lower rewards for their services. If sufficient cuts are made A and B goods output may be increased by the full amount of the indemnity, and if that happens the unemployment will disappear. How drastic the cuts required are will depend largely on the elasticity of demand and supply of the country's goods ; the greater the elasticity the smaller the cuts required.[1] It will also depend on the nature of the exports. If they consist largely of B goods, more drastic cuts will probably be required than if they consisted largely of A goods. For the indemnity payment shifts the demand for goods in general from the tax-payers of the paying country to the tax-payers of the receiving country. This shift in demand will tend to give the producers of competing B goods in the indemnity receiving country a marketing advantage over those in the indemnity paying country.[2] Thus the paying country will have to cut the price of its B goods relatively to that of the receiving country's B goods by a sufficient amount, which may be large, to tempt buyers in the receiving country to transfer their demand from their home-made goods, to which they are accustomed, to unwonted foreign-made goods of different pattern.[3] Thus the factors in the paying country will have to reduce their rewards more and the price of the output will have to fall more in the case of B than in that of

[1] Cf. the analysis of ch. II, pp. 31–35. [2] Cf. p. 112.

[3] This will be further accentuated, if the receiving country imposes a tariff.

A goods. As against this it must be remarked that the production of B goods is more likely to show decreasing costs over a considerable range, resulting from the larger market.

Thus the burden of an indemnity is twofold. The paying country has to reduce its expenditure by an amount equal to the taxation required to cover the indemnity. In addition it must either allow an unemployment crisis to persist, with the resulting loss of output and income, or it must reduce the real reward to factors of production.

A reduction in F, whether due to the necessity to make an indemnity payment, to a loss of interest on foreign investments, etc., will give rise to transitional problems similar to those following the loss of a foreign market. An initial passive balance of payments is to be expected and some measure of internal deflation by the central bank. In the absence of counteracting causes, the unemployment will not be a transitional but a permanent phenomenon.

§ 4. *International Capital Movements.* It is required to define the equilibrium position when capital movements are taken into account. In this position the foreign balance on all current items is equal to the net foreign lending of the country, and the all foreign payments balance exactly. In a period of normal advance there may indeed be some active balance of an amount equal to the share of newly mined gold which the country acquires.

The figure for the net foreign lending is found by subtracting long and short term loans made by foreigners to the country from long and short term loans made by the country to foreigners. The volume of long term capital movements depends on the prospects of profit in industry at home together with the amount of government and municipal development loans issued, on the powers of the country by saving to satisfy its own capital needs (these two factors determining the rate of interest and profit in the country) on the relation of these to interest and profit obtainable elsewhere, and on the comparative confidence in the stability and future progress of the country. The volume of short term loans is determined in part by similar considerations but also largely by the policy of the central bank.[1]

It may be well to consider the allocation of income, when capital movements are taken into account. The income of the community is derived from the sale of A, B and C goods, including capital goods, and from the " other " current items on the foreign balance-sheet. Its allocation is divided between expenditure on A, B and C consumable goods, " other " current items on the foreign balance sheet and unconsumed income.[2] The component parts of income and its allocation may be sorted out in such a way that their common items can be cancelled.

[1] In abnormal times like the present, the policy of the central bank and government has also a large influence on the volume of long term lending.

[2] In this analysis the whole income of a firm operating in England is said to accrue to the English community ; that part of it set aside to reserve is " unconsumed income " ; that part paid out to foreign partners or shareholders is an item of disbursement in the " other " current items on the foreign balance-sheet.

The expression " unconsumed income " is used in the sense commonly given to the word " savings." Mr. Keynes has, however, recently defined savings in a somewhat different sense, and to avoid confusion that term is not used in the text.

INCOME	ALLOCATION

1. Value of all consumable goods sold in home market. = 1. Value of all consumable goods bought in home market.

2. Value of exports =
   (i) Balance of trade.[1]
   +(ii) Value of consumable goods imported.
   +(iii) Value of capital goods imported.
   = 2. Value of consumable goods bought from abroad.

3. Value of newly produced capital goods made and sold at home.

4. Income from " other " current items on foreign balance-sheet =
   (i) Balance of other current items on foreign balance-sheet.[1]
   +(ii) Income devoted to other current items on foreign balance-sheet.
   = 3. Income devoted to other current items on foreign balance-sheet.

4. Unconsumed income.

Eliminating common items there is left, on one side, the balance of all foreign items on current account and the value of the addition to the home stock of capital goods, and on the other unconsumed income.

In equilibrium the balance of all items on current account is equal to net foreign lending ; consequently net

---

[1] This item may have a negative value.

foreign lending plus the addition to the home stock of capital goods is equal to unconsumed income.

Let an equilibrium position be disturbed by the opening of a new field for profitable foreign lending.[1] In the new equilibrium this new lending must be offset either by a reduction in the addition to the home stock of capital goods or by an increase of unconsumed income, or by both. Neither adjustment can be made without some disturbance occurring in the whole economic system.

In the first instance, before repercussions are allowed for, there will be a net passive balance equal to the amount of new foreign lending. How is this covered ?

The most complete adjustment will be secured if, simultaneously with the increase of lending, rewards to factors are cut sufficiently to stimulate the output of A and B goods by enough to cover the passive balance. This does not imply an increase of A and B output by an amount equal to the new lending, but a greater increase. For part of the income of the newly employed factors will be expended on A and B purchases ; and the part of their new income not so expended will give additional employment to C producers, who will also expend part of their income on A and B purchases. Rewards to factors must therefore be reduced sufficiently to stimulate A and B output so much that the increase of A and B sales less the consequential increase of A and

[1] Equilibrium may also be disturbed by an increase in the addition to the home stock of capital goods ; if these are imported the effect on the foreign balance will be direct, if they are home-made it will be indirect through the increased purchases of A and B goods by those earning income in the home capital goods trades ; the effect of this on the balance may be important and necessitate adjustments analogous to those discussed in the text.

B purchases is equal to the new foreign lending. This in turn will be equal to the increase of unconsumed income in the new equilibrium. When the new foreign lending is due, to an increase of lendable funds consequent upon a general expansion of output and income and increase of efficiency at home, this type of adjustment is usually the one that occurs. The reduction of home efficiency rewards is then constituted not by a fall in money rewards but by a rise in efficiency. The new foreign lending is associated with a concomitant increase of unconsumed income ; this increase may well exceed the new foreign lending, which is consequently accompanied by a rise and not a fall in the addition to the home stock of capital goods.

It is necessary to examine the case in which the new foreign lending is not accompanied by a reduction of efficiency rewards. (The following reasoning applies *mutatis mutandis* when there is a moderate but insufficient reduction of efficiency rewards.)

(i) If the new flow of foreign lending ($=\pounds p$) is found by an increase of the margin between income and expenditure on consumable goods (an increase of unconsumed income), we may suppose that the purchase of A and B goods is cut down by $\pounds q_1$, and that of C goods by $\pounds p - q_1$. So far there is a net passive balance of $\pounds p - q_1$. We must suppose that the reduction in C incomes of $\pounds p - q_1$ entails a corresponding reduction of expenditure on consumable goods. For otherwise the initial supposition that the new funds for foreign lending are found wholly by increasing the margin between income and expenditure will not be fulfilled. The opposite case is examined in the following paragraph. Suppose an additional reduction of the purchase of A and B consumables of $\pounds q_2$ and consequently a further transfer of reduction on C consumables of $£p-(q_1+q_2)$. On the supposition that the margin between income and expenditure is maintained, there will be a progressive transfer of reduction in C incomes, until there is no more to transfer, i.e. until $q_1+q_2+\ldots=p$, i.e. until the reduction in A and B consumption is equal to the new foreign lending. The consequence of the new foreign lending will have been to reduce C incomes by $£\left(\dfrac{1}{h}\right)p$, where h is the proportion of income, formerly but no longer expended, which was devoted to the purchase of A and B goods. Analysis of what may happen in the transition is on precisely the same lines as when a foreign market worth $£p$ has been lost (*vid. sup.*[1]).[2]

(ii) Suppose on the other hand that the additional flow of foreign lending is accompanied by no increase of unconsumed income. This is the opposite extreme; the actual condition is likely to be intermediate. The force which on the other hypothesis tended to diffuse unemployment, namely, the reduction of expenditure on C consumables, will not at once come into operation. There will in the first instance be an uncovered passive balance. What will the new equilibrium be? When that is

---

[1] Pp. 110–113.

[2] In this paragraph it has been assumed that there is no reduction in the rate of addition to the stock of capital goods. If, however, the reduced output $(£p-q_1)$ of C consumables entails reduced demand for (and output of) capital goods at home, of which r_1 were of the A and B class, and if the expenditure on A and B goods of factors so thrown out of work in C capital goods industries was s_1, the total net reduction in the purchase of A and B goods in the first term of the series is $(q_1+r_1+s_1)$. Production in all C industries will decrease until $(q_1+r_1+s_1)+(q_2+r_2+s_2)+\ldots=p$.

achieved, the trade balance will have been raised sufficiently to cover the new flow of foreign lending. It may happen that the investment is of a kind which gives the lending country a competing advantage in the sale of certain B goods, e.g. machinery, locomotives, etc., to the market in which the new investment is being made, and the passive balance will be partly covered in this way. The whole passive balance is not likely to be so covered. It is necessary to advert to the policy of the central bank. It may be able to cover the passive balance out of its reserves. As it loses reserves, it may either neutralize the effect of the loss by purchasing securities in the open market and so maintaining the quantity of money in the country at its old level, or it may allow the outflow of reserves to have its direct effect of reducing the bankers' balances.

If it pursues the former policy it is really counting on a further change occurring. It may hope that the stimulus to new foreign lending will spend itself quickly, or that an improvement in foreign markets will occur, allowing an increase in the trade balance. It can pursue such a waiting policy with greater equanimity if its reserves are very large. If on the other hand it allows the outflow to have its full effect on bankers' balances, the banks will have to curtail their loans and interest rates will rise. This has the short period effect of inducing a reverse flow of short term loans to the country and the more far-reaching effect of checking the output of capital goods for the home market.[1] This creates unemployment

---

[1] A high interest rate reduces the present value of a given prospective income and so checks the output of capital goods. The reduction of capital goods includes any reduction in liquid or working capital that may occur.

in the capital goods industries, which diffuses unemployment, on the principle already explained, in the domestic consumable goods industries and reduces the purchase of A and B goods. So long as the cash basis is in the process of being reduced (by a passive balance), the rising tendency of rates will continue; this will diffuse unemployment in the capital goods industries and the C consumables industries, until the purchase of A and B goods is reduced by the amount of the net addition to foreign lending. At that point the contraction of loans will cease and with it the contraction of capital construction. Sufficient unemployment will have been created to generate an active trade balance, through the fall in income reducing the purchase of A and B goods by an amount equal to the new foreign lending.

The central bank may have to take still more drastic action. If it feels itself unable to cover the passive balance which is generated in the first instance, it may be impelled to accelerate the process of contraction by contracting its own credit. If the proportion of its reserves to liabilities is to be restored to its level in the old equilibrium, some contraction of central bank credit will in any case be necessary.

A similar analysis applies in the case of a country which having been on balance a borrowing country finds itself cut off from foreign loans. When loans cease or are reduced, the passive trade balance exceeds the net inflow of capital and the position is consequently one of disequilibrium. There will be an outflow of money and the central bank is faced with a problem similar to that already discussed.

In a time of normal advance the increase in a country's lending may not do more than keep pace with her rising output of A and B goods and her rising efficiency. The loans do indeed check the rate at which internal advance is possible, but they build up a strong position in the future for her, and their rising yield promotes internal prosperity. Such was roughly the course of this country's foreign lending before the war. It is arguable that in the post-war decade she clung too tenaciously to her lending habit in a period when for various reasons her A and B output was checked in its normal rate of expansion, and that unemployment and depression in the country would have been less, had she lent less.

In abnormal times big changes may occur in the item of foreign lending. A country's power to borrow may suddenly cease owing to a loss of confidence of foreigners in her or to convulsions proceeding elsewhere. Or her own lending may increase owing to her nationals' loss of confidence (" flight of capital "). Her own increase of lending could not, it is true, be long maintained on a great scale, since it must be derived either from unconsumed income or from the monetary balances of nationals which they are willing to trench on for this purpose. The first source will shrivel up in the crisis which a large uncovered passive balance must engender at home, while the second can be drawn on once only. None the less any country may experience a large temporary increase in her passive balance owing to an increase of her foreign lending, and a borrowing country may experience a large permanent increase, so long as her power to attract loans is in suspense. When this occurs the diffusion of unemployment required to reduce her A and B purchases by the amount necessary to secure a new equilibrium may be exceedingly great, involving a paralysis of her whole economic life. In such a situation it may be necessary to control all dealings in foreign exchange or to abandon the gold standard.

§ 5.   *The Balance of Payments and Deflation.*   The following changes in fundamental conditions all tending to generate a passive balance in the first instance have been passed in review in the preceding sections : (i) the loss of some advantage in the sphere of comparative costs entailing a reduction of exports ; (ii) a fall in the world price level unaccompanied by a *pari passu* reduction of inflexible efficiency-rewards at home (or a rise in efficiency-rewards at home unaccompanied by a rise in the world price level) ; (iii) a rise in the proportion of income devoted to the purchase of A and B goods (*h*) ; (iv) a reduction in the net income from other items in the balance of payments on current account, due to such causes as a fall in income from foreign investments or the necessity to make an indemnity payment and (v) an increase in the net flow of foreign lending. The opposite circumstances would generate an active balance in the first instance.   At any time there may well be factors operating in both directions and offsetting each other, as, for instance, when the proportion of expenditure devoted to the purchase of A and B goods is falling and the net flow of foreign lending is increasing.   A passive (or active) balance may indeed occur when none of these factors are present, being due to seasonal or transitory causes. Such discrepancies may be covered out of the reserve of the central bank or by its operating on the market rate of discount to induce offsetting changes in the flow of short term loans.

A change in the fundamental conditions tending in the first instance to generate a passive balance entails a reduction of the total income of the community when a new equilibrium is reached. This reduction is likely also to involve a fall in the amount of money which the community collectively chooses to hold ; consequently in the transition between the two equilibria there must be a net passive balance or internal deflation (contraction of bank loans) or both. If the central bank's proportion of reserve to liabilities is to be restored to its old level, there must be some internal deflation ; the proportion of the reduction in the total monetary holding of the community which is covered by a passive balance and by internal deflation respectively must be equal to the proportion of the central bank's reserves to the total monetary holdings of the community.

In a modern community the banking system performs two main functions, it provides a circulating medium in the form of bank notes and bank deposits and it provides the capital market with funds. These two functions are inextricably intertwined. It cannot cancel part of the circulating medium without withdrawing funds from the capital market. Thus if the monetary requirements of the community are falling by an amount that is greater than can conveniently be covered by a passive balance (which involves depletion of banking reserves) and it is necessary to resort to internal deflation, the banking system has to withdraw funds from the capital market. Deflation operates through a rise of interest rates and a consequent fall in the output of capital goods. To examine the interaction between changes in the monetary requirements of a community (involving creation and cancellation of means of payment) and changes in the equilibrium rate of output of capital goods would take us to the heart of the problem of the trade

cycle.   This is largely an unsolved one, and certain
generalities must suffice here.

In an equilibrium position the proportion of the
community's factors devoted to adding to the stock of
capital goods should be equal to the proportion of consumer's incomes which they choose not to spend, less
the net foreign lending ($=$the active balance of payments
on current account).   The equilibrium rate of interest
(or, more strictly, series of interest rates, for there are
different rates appropriate to different classes and periods
of loan) is that which limits the demand for new capital
goods to this proportion.   If the banking system aims
at securing such a rate, the volume of loans, to which
it finds itself committed as a consequence, should be just
sufficient to provide the community with the means of
payment it requires, either a stable amount or one rising
in accordance with a normal long period trend.[1]   Consequently when equilibrium is reached after a change in
the community's external relations represented in its
balance of payments, the banking policy appropriate
to its monetary requirements in the new phase should
not be inconsistent with that required to secure an
equilibrium rate of output of new capital goods.   It is
more difficult to write with certainty of the appropriate
behaviour in the transition period.   Measures required
to secure an appropriate contraction of the circulating
medium may entail an excessive contraction of capital
output.   Moreover, it appeared above that in the transi-

---

[1] This amount may, however, have to fluctuate to offset
variations in the tendency to hoard due to psychological or
other causes, if these persist, as they may prove to, in an otherwise steadily advancing community (*vid. inf.* ch. VIII, pp.
162–164).

tion the passive balance may tend to exceed the amount required to reduce the circulating medium from its level in the old to that in the new equilibrium, and the dose of deflation required would then be *pro tanto* stronger.

Analysis appears to show that it is possible for a closed community to become involved in a vicious circle of inflation or deflation. Expansion of output is indeed restricted by the limit of what is physically possible, but there is no such limit to a recession. A new equilibrium may be found at a low level of output with a small proportion of productive factors devoted to capital goods. In an open system, e.g. in a particular country with external trading relations, the level of output is determined, as already explained, by the relation of efficiency rewards to world prices, the proportion of income devoted to the purchase of world goods and the size of the other items in the foreign balance-sheet. If the deflation, necessitated during a transitition, tended to push the production of capital goods and C consumables in that country below the level so determined, an active balance would ultimately be generated and recuperative forces would be set in motion tending to revive output. This, however, is not quite the end of the matter.

The world as a whole *is* a closed system. If output in the world as a whole is receding owing to the prevalence of deflation, the level of the output at which each country achieves equilibrium will recede also. It might be thought that a change in the balance of payments necessitating deflationary measures in one country would normally be accompanied by a change necessitating inflationary measures in another and that mere movements in the balance should not engender inflation or deflation in the world as a whole. There may be some truth in this ; it may be that we must look elsewhere for causes tending to produce world expansions and recessions. This much, however, may be observed here. An active balance does not exert as strong a coercive force on a central bank to adapt its monetary policy to the situation as a passive balance does. A passive balance must be checked or insolvency will result ; a rise in the proportion of a central bank's reserve due to an active balance may be endured with equanimity. It is not improbable therefore that adjustments of banking policy due to changes in the balance of payments may involve some measure of net deflation in the world as a whole. It would follow that there may well be some truth in the view that the greater violence of the changes in the balance of payments, which for various reasons have prevailed in recent years, is a contributory cause of the greater failure of world output to keep pace with the capacity of productive factors. If the forces of deflation prevail over those of inflation on balance in the first instance, and a world recession ensues, the world as a whole may enter into the vicious circle of deflation and deflationary conditions be extended to all countries.

Some remarks may be made on certain palliatives, which are apt to be adopted in the face of a world recession. One is the imposition by particular countries of additional tariffs, import quotas or exchange restrictions. In a general retreat some countries may be peculiarly exposed and their equilibrium level of output be reduced to a fantastically low level. By protecting the home market for their A and B output, they may enable some production still to be undertaken.[1] Desperate measures

[1] On the general question of the relation of a tariff to employment, see ch. IX, sec. 4.

of salvage may be necessary. Two points may be made about this remedy : (i) Prima facie, what is gained at home is lost in the outer world, since the balance of trade of the outer world with the restricting country is rendered less favourable. There may, however, be some net gain. If some of the countries which suffer by the import restrictions are those with an active balance, their rate of recession may not be so much accelerated by the loss, as the recession of the ill-placed countries is retarded by their salvage measures. For a relatively strong country to impose restrictions in a time of world recession is inexcusable. (ii) The restrictions, so long as they are in force, make revival more difficult, since the channels in which the reviving trade will have to flow are less profitable than those blocked up.

An especially ill-placed country may seek to raise loans from her stronger neighbours. While the loan is flowing in, her equilibrium level of output is raised by an amount equal to the loan multiplied by $\frac{1}{h}$. The net effect on the world level of output depends on how the loan is raised. If it entails a corresponding reduction in the *output* of capital goods in the lending country and of her *purchase* of consumable goods it has no restorative effect. If on the other hand it can be provided without either of these consequences ensuing, it will tend to arrest the process of world recession. This implies that the lending country can allow her active balance to be reduced or her passive balance increased by the full amount of the loan. One further point may be made in this connection. If, instead of making the loan of £p, the strong country increased her *own* output of capital goods sufficiently to raise her purchase of world goods

K

by £p the result would be still more satisfactory. In both cases the outer world's balance of payments with the strong country would rise by £p. Whereas in the former case an additional (interest) charge is put upon the already distressed industries or governments of the weak countries and the money is used to cover the losses of unprofitable trade, in the latter case the incoming money represents the yield of trade now rendered profitable. The strong country also gains by the latter method since it increases her own consumption and employment. Nothing can be more foolish than to make distress loans to an impoverished country while maintaining a tariff against her goods or while reducing expenditure on development at home.

If the regime of stable exchanges is abandoned, the mechanism by which the transition is made from one equilibrium to another is different ; in particular, when an adverse turn occurs, deflation can be avoided. In certain circumstances the regime of stable exchanges may indeed have a stabilizing influence ; it prevents countries which are parties to it from indulging in private orgies of inflation or deflation, because under it those are checked by the passive or active balances generated in consequence of them. But when the position is reversed and big changes in the balance occurring for other reasons necessitate large measures of internal inflation or deflation to counteract them, and when in consequence there is a tendency for the forces of deflation to exceed those of inflation in the world as a whole, it is proper to examine the possibilities of the other system. This is done in the following chapter. Then, in Chapter VIII, the possibility of retaining the advantages of stable or fairly stable exchanges, while avoiding inflation or deflation in the world as a whole, through international co-operation, is considered.

CHAPTER VII

WHEN THE GOLD STANDARD IS ABANDONED

§ 1. *The New Freedom.* In an earlier chapter the reader was asked to bear in his mind two distinct problems : (i) What are the circumstances in which a country will distribute her productive resources among occupation in the best possible manner ? (ii) What are the circumstances in which a country will make a full use of her productive resources ? The first problem was considered in Chapters II and III. In Chapter IV it appeared that full use of productive resources depended on rewards to factors being in a given relation to the world level of prices. In the last chapter it was shown that, if these rewards were not readily adjustable, any force tending to generate a passive balance in the first instance is likely to disseminate unemployment in the country. Furthermore the passive balance will, if considerable, necessitate some measure of internal deflation, entailing a further addition to unemployment in the transition and a more lasting further addition if the world generally becomes infected with deflation. The original passive balance might be due to a change in the relative position of the country or, again, to the prevalence of deflation in the world as a whole.

If the monetary authority is not obliged to maintain

the foreign exchange rates at a fixed par and does not attempt to do so, the scene is greatly changed. A new freedom is gained. This may be most precisely demonstrated by reference to the terms in our equilibrium equation for simplified conditions :

$$I = \frac{1}{h}(I_t)$$

What have been referred to in these pages as the " fundamental conditions " no longer serve to determine the terms in this equation. These conditions are : (i) the efficiency rewards of home factors of production ; (ii) the external price level ; and (iii) the tastes of spenders at home. So long as a gold standard is postulated, or any form of stable exchange rates with the currencies of other countries, I_t, the value of A and B output which producers find it profitable to turn out, given home efficiency rewards and the external price level, is determined. But if the rate at which the home currency exchanges for foreign currency is undetermined, this quantity, I_t, is undetermined also. And if I_t is undetermined, so too is I.

When a force begins to operate which would in a regime of stable exchanges, tend to depress I_t, the monetary authorities consisting of the central bank and the government, can take action to maintain I_t at its old level. This will involve such revaluation of the home currency in terms of other currencies as is required to keep the relation of home efficiency rewards to world prices in a full-employment position. Both unemployment and deflation can be avoided. This reasoning applies, *mutatis mutandis*, when there are other items in the foreign balance of payments.

So long as the monetary policy of the country is indeterminate, the effect of any given change on the employment position cannot be determined. It may happen that the monetary authorities have no view as to what ought to be done or consciousness of their own power. They must, however, do something, they must behave in a certain manner, the government with regard to its borrowing and sinking fund, the bank with regard to its bank rate and loan policy ; and their actions will, however unintentionally, determine the issue. The government may wash its hands of the matter and declare that it will let the exchange find its natural level ; but there is no natural level ! There are an infinite number of possible levels. The level will be precisely determined by what the government and bank do. They may have no specific policy, but they cannot do nothing. Their behaviour may be actuated by irrelevant, subsidiary or even trifling motives ; none the less it will decide that vitally important question, what the output and income of the community is to be.

The power of the authorities is both more formidable and somewhat more limited than has so far been explained. It is more formidable because, in determining the foreign exchange rates, they also indirectly fix the real value or purchasing power of rewards to factors. It is more limited because, if their policy produced a big change in the real value of these rewards, pressure might be brought to bear to alter the rewards with success. A large downward movement in the exchange rates, for instance, altering the relation of efficiency rewards at home to world prices, might be countered by a rise in money rewards at home, by which the old relation would be restored.

The use of their powers must no doubt involve the authorities in complicated problems concerning both the general good and equity between different interests. None the less it ought not to be too optimistic to hope that some intelligent attempt to use it would produce better results than the policy of the ostrich. Let us revoke this power, it might be urged, as quickly as possible and return to the gold standard. This, unfortunately, would by itself be no solution. For the course of world gold prices, which has so much effect for good or ill on the domestic situation, and which we have so far considered for convenience in discussing the equilibrium in a particular country to be " given," a decree of fate, is not in fact a decree of fate, but results from the action of a number of ostriches, the governments and central banks of the different countries. It may well prove easier for one government to make an intelligent use of its own powers, than to persuade the whole collection to do so in concert. For the use of this power necessarily involves new and untried measures. The *only* well-tried expedient is *laissez-faire ;* most of the authorities, who think about the matter at all, probably continue to hope against hope that the old expedient will still serve. Their hope is not likely to be realized.

§ 2. *Stabilizing the Value of Money. The Objective.* There will of necessity be a larger speculative element in the discussions which follow than in those which have preceded. In the past countries which have had to depart from the gold standard have done so as the result of a strong internal inflation, and analysis of a regime of paper money has tended to concern itself with inflationary conditions. The present situation in which a number of

countries have departed from the gold standard in a time
of deep deflation, a deflation by no means terminated
even for them by that departure, is essentially novel.[1]
It is consequently proper to review the situation in more
general terms.

The whole question is so indeterminate, as not to be
amenable to analysis, unless we suppose some specific
attitude to the situation on the part of the authorities.
Let us suppose that in the initial position factors are
fully employed, with due allowance, of course, for unemployment due to seasonal causes, normal shifts in demand
between commodities, the reserve of labour, etc., and
that the authorities determine upon a course of action,
which appeals to common sense, namely, to keep the
purchasing power of the domestic money stable in terms
of A and B commodities.

If they do this, *and there is no change in the relevant
special circumstances*, the full employment position will be
maintained, however foreign prices behave. A rise or
fall in the open-market world price level will at once be
countered by a rise or fall in the foreign exchange rates,
so that the relation between home efficiency rewards and
world prices will be maintained at a constant level. This
policy may be justified not only as a common-sense one,
but also as avoiding the difficult problem as to whether
the government ought to make itself responsible for
altering real rewards to factors by its monetary policy.
Such a policy would not entail altering real rewards.

It is now incumbent upon us to make an exhaustive
examination of the changes in the " relevant circumstances " which might, even if this policy were pursued,

[1] Cf. G. Cassel, *Rhodes Lectures*, 1932 : " The Crisis in the
World's Monetary System," p. 34.

disturb the maintenance of the country's activity at a full level. These are : (i) changes in the prices of particular A and B goods ; (ii) changes in efficiency at home ; (iii) changes in rewards at home (changes under either (ii) or (iii) constitute changes in " efficiency rewards ") ; (iv) changes in h ; (v) changes in the size of the home population or, more generally, the amount of factors available for employment ; (vi) changes of " other " items in the foreign balance on current account or in the net movement of foreign lending ; and (vii) a very important matter, which will be explained later, a shrinkage in foreign markets, contradistinguished from a fall in the foreign price level.

(i) It is possible that, while sterling is held stable in terms of commodities generally, the prices of the goods in which we have a comparative advantage might fall relatively to prices generally. The sterling prices of such goods would then, under this policy, fall absolutely, and our output of A and B goods would be restricted. Unemployment and diminished profits would be disseminated accordingly. It is not clear what policy such an eventuality calls for. The root fact is that the gain available from foreign trade has been reduced by the changed conditions outside. The efficiency of our people measured in physical output has not indeed fallen, but measured in world values it has. They can get less of what they want by exchange in return for their work than they could before. It follows that *either* the community must be willing to endure a certain amount of unemployment, thus artificially, as it were, maintaining their efficiency at its old level by confining their endeavours to fields where their efficiency is greatest,[1] *or* rewards to

[1] Cf. ch. IV, sec. 5, p. 75.

factors must be reduced. Whether the government should secure an automatic reduction in the rewards, by depressing the exchanges and lowering the purchasing power of sterling in terms of world commodities, thus maintaining full employment, or leave unemployment to run its course and rewards to be reduced, if at all, by private negotiation, I leave as an open question. At a time like the present, when real productive potentiality is rising rapidly—a potentiality which would become actual under sound monetary conditions—it is probable that this particular adverse factor would be offset by other favourable circumstances, and no net reduction would be needed.

(ii) Changes of efficiency at home, measured in physical terms,[1] are likely on balance to be in a favourable direction. *Ceteris paribus*, A and B output would expand accordingly, and the total national income would rise. If, as supposed, initial employment was full, there would be no room for further employment. Profits would become inflated. There would be a proper pressure to raise rewards to factors. If rewards were raised precisely in proportion to increased efficiency, the *status quo* would be maintained. It is arguable that, in the case of rewards being raised insufficiently, or of a considerable lag in their adjustment, the government should raise the external value of sterling, that is, increase its power of purchasing world goods. Such action would only be justified if it was clear that employment was as full as the incidence of normal changes and dislocations allows us to expect it can be, and that efficiency had gone ahead of rewards,

---

[1] The possibility of a reduction of value as opposed to reduction of volume per unit of effort is precisely the eventuality mentioned in the last paragraph.

profits being inflated. Whether the government should allow the profit inflation to rip, or counter it by raising the value of the currency, I must again leave as an open question for the present. It will recur in the discussion of world monetary reform.

(iii) Changes in rewards proportional to changes in efficiency have already been discussed. If there is a successful movement to raise rewards exceeding the improvement in efficiency, the problem is a more delicate one. It might be held that in the old equilibrium certain classes were receiving an inadequate share of the product of industry and that profit makers and *rentiers* should in equity be squeezed. If profits really can be squeezed, in the sense that after the squeeze production proceeds as before, well and good. But if A and B output falls off, and other output consequentially, the wage earners or other classes whose rates of pay have been raised, will themselves be damaged. It would have been better to effect the redistribution, if called for in equity, by more progressive taxation or other means. However misguided the policy of securing the improvement may have been, it is doubtful whether the government ought to counter it by changing the value of money. Nothing could be more undesirable than a race between wages and prices. There seems nothing for it but to let the unemployment due to the rise in rewards endure. It should probably be accepted as a rule that the government should make no attempt to reduce the value of the currency in terms of world goods at a time when a general rise in unadjustable monetary rewards is occurring. The policy of stability should then be maintained.

(iv) A rise in h means, *ceteris paribus*, that output and income will be restricted, and a fall means the opposite.

Any change of this sort is likely to be a small amount per annum. If, however, the tendency were all in one direction and the scene otherwise peaceful, the cumulative effects might be large and the inflationary or deflationary conditions engendered severe. Should the government take countervailing measures? I think so. If the shift was towards A and B goods, the purchasing power of sterling should be lowered. Since the shift is voluntary, the consumers are presumably benefiting themselves by making it, and it is only right that they should pay an enhanced price for the preferred class of goods. If the shift is towards C consumables, it spreads employment and prosperity at home and consumers might be allowed to get their A and B goods more cheaply, to induce them not to make such a large shift to C goods as to engender inflationary conditions at home.

In the normal advance of society the shift is likely to be towards C goods,[1] and the appropriate countervailing measure a rise in the value of the currency. The reader of puritan temper may find consolation in the fact that of the circumstances so far considered the only two held likely to be normal or recurrent require deflationary and not inflationary intervention by the authorities. The authorities might find some difficulty in computing h from the statistical material at present at their disposal.[2]

---

[1] For reasons, see ch. III, pp. 52-54.

[2] A fall in h might be due to an increase of unconsumed income; in this case the central bank must encourage the construction of capital goods, so as to increase their output by an equivalent amount. Such an " easy money " policy would not depress the foreign exchange rates, but only prevent their rising by as much as they would otherwise tend to owing to the diminished purchase of imports (fall in h).

(v) Increments of population will not find employment unless A and B output expands. If the growth is accompanied by an improvement in efficiency and especially if the conditions of supply are elastic, so that a small improvement makes a large expansion of output possible, there will be no problem. Otherwise, we shall be in the presence of the phenomenon of Diminishing Returns or over-population. What should be the attitude of the government ? Some might urge that it should attack the disease and not the symptoms, and confine its activity to restricting the population ! This question is outside the subject of this volume. It is likely also to be an academic one for some time to come in countries with fully developed economic systems, for they are due to enter a long period of declining populations.[1] Increments of savings or enterprise may be expected to find employment through a decline in their offer price. The maintenance of interest rates by the banking system appropriate to the flow of saving should not be inconsistent with a stable money policy.[2]

(vi) A decline of other items in the foreign balance will create unemployment unless it is accompanied by a reduction in the value of the currency. In normal times these changes proceed slowly. Sharp changes may come about in the form of nations being compelled to make large reparation or indemnity payments. The world has now presumably learned its lesson that these should be eschewed. Big capital movements may arise out of a loss of confidence in a country's currency. Such a loss would not be likely to

[1] Unless a spectacular rise in birth rates occurs, which does not seem indicated by present social tendencies.

[2] Cf. ch. VI, sec. 5, p. 132.

happen if it was subject to the management here proposed. Substantial changes in these items in the foreign balance may none the less occur ; capital may be drawn out by a boom proceeding in another country ; the yield of foreign investments may fail owing to world depression. A tempting solution is for the government to obtain control over foreign investment ; this course is, however, beset with grave practical difficulties. A distinction must be drawn between changes in the balance destined to be permanent and big particular movements. The former are like to be gradual and to be offset by other changes in the general situation discussed in these paragraphs. It would probably be unwise to change the value of the currency to offset a big particular movement. It is probably better to suffer a period of unemployment. The authorities must be careful to keep that unemployment within the limits warranted by the occasion and not to allow any tendency for the currency to appreciate in terms of commodities to take effect. Even the troubles due to big movements are ultimately susceptible of remedy, namely, by international co-operation ; for the big movements are usually due to currency mismanagement *somewhere*.

(vii) If none of the changes referred to in the foregoing paragraphs occur and the value of the domestic currency is left stable in terms of world commodities, full production must, it might appear, be maintained. All the A and B output that was feasible initially will continue to be feasible and, h being stable, the total output of the community will bear the same relation to A and B output as before. Suppose, it might be objected, that the obnoxious practice of hoarding sets in. The authorities, pledged to prevent the value of the currency rising, will *ex hypothesei* have countered this by inflationary measures. Yet there is still one difficulty.

This difficulty would not occur if all the A and B output of the country was A output. If the prices of A goods and their costs of production remain the same, nothing can prevent the country from continuing the production of these goods at the old rate. But this is not altogether true of B goods, in which the world market is incompletely organized. If the world demand for an A commodity shrinks and its gold price falls, but its sterling price does not fall, England will continue to produce as much as before, and that means that she will satisfy a larger proportion of the world demand than before. This will entail a further fall of world prices and other producers may complain of dumping. The more fools they, for allowing their own process of deflation to go forward! In the case of B goods the invasion of competitors' markets is not quite so simple. England's currency authority provides that the average price of B goods in the world expressed in sterling is the same as before. It does not follow that English exporters will still be able to sell as much as they can produce at the old sterling price.

Is the currency authority to assist them by reducing exchange rates still further? There is much to be said on both sides. To some extent the B producers can help themselves; just because their market is not organized they may be able to extend their sales by offering goods at lower prices in the sections where they are invading competitors' markets; the fall in the exchange, which we postulate as occurring anyhow, will give them some competitive advantage. The strong argument against assisting them further is that it may involve reducing the purchasing power of money and consequently rewards to factors. It involves compelling factors to bear the brunt of the world crisis in the form of reduced rewards instead of unemployment; it is arguable that they should be allowed to choose this for themselves. On the other side it could be represented to the factors that the extra rise of prices was for the duration of the crisis only; in a time of world crisis it is vitally important that the country should not become infected with the deflationary mentality, which will probably be rife in the world; unemployment and business losses are more favourable conditions for the spread of the disease than a moderate rise in the cost of living; the stronger policy of depressing sterling further is also valuable as a demonstration to the outer world.

It might be objected that the policy of maintaining the quantum of exports is predatory *vis-à-vis* other countries seeking markets for similar goods. They would only have themselves to blame for allowing deflation in their own country; it is good that they should be shaken out of their rut; but more will be said about the predatory aspect of a stable currency policy in times of slump in the next section; much depends on the means by which it is carried out. This question may also be left open; there is certainly a case for the view that a country (like England) whose tradable output is mainly B should raise her general index of A and B prices somewhat during a period of world slump.

To summarize the conclusions of this section, it is clear that the proposed policy of maintaining a stable A-and-B price level would do much to maintain output at a full level. If none of the seven changes discussed in this section occurred it would maintain it at as full a level as can be expected in the most favourable circumstances. Of the possible changes, those envisaged as probable in sub-sections (ii) and (iv) indicated that a gradual long-period downward trend of prices might well prove desirable in an advancing community. In sub-section (vi) it appeared that violent movements in the non-trading part of the foreign balance-sheet might set up adverse repercussions which it would be very difficult to counter. In sub-section (vii) it was suggested that, in a period of world slump, some rise in A and B prices expressed in the home currency for the duration of the slump might be desirable for a country whose output was largely of the B type.

The whole argument of this section has been based on the assumption that at the starting point employment was at a high level. To inaugurate the policy when production was at a low level during a depression, would, by a parity of reasoning, prolong the depression indefinitely. The policy must be inaugurated when employment is full. If it is not full, steps must first be taken to improve the situation.

Deflationists sometimes argue that the only way to avoid a slump is to prevent the preceding boom. It is better to say that the only way to avoid a slump is to engineer a boom. If a slump has occurred and no boom is allowed to occur, prosperity can never return. A boom may be defined as an increase in the rate of output which *cannot* be maintained in the long period. Prosperity may be defined as a condition in which output is at a level which involves reasonably full use of the productive resources available and is increasing at a rate which *can* be maintained in the long period. If depression is to give place to prosperity, there must be an intervening period of boom. For if output is initially low, in relation to capacity, and it is never allowed to advance at a rate " which cannot be maintained in the long period," it must remain permanently below that which involves " a reasonably full use of productive resources." And it must remain permanently as far below what is reasonably possible as it is initially. Stabilization should be introduced after and not before the boom. But, it will be objected, it is wrong to stabilize after a boom, because the boom-process is apt to make the development of particular industries lop-sided. But so also is the slump-process ! Whenever stabilization is undertaken there will be some lop-sidedness as between particular industries initially. That will tend to get straightened out in time. What is important is that the stabilization should occur when the average level of output is high. To propose stabilization after a severe slump is merely lunatic. Reflationary measures are then necessary as a precursor of price stabilization.

§ 3. *Stabilizing the Value of Money. The Means.* In the last section we have been concerned with the objectived of currency policy ; there was no reference to the means by which it may be achieved. In order to understand the means aright it may be of assistance to make an excursion into the question of what would happen in a regime of complete *laissez-faire*. It has already been explained that this concept is hardly susceptible of analysis, since both the bank and government must do something, even if their motives are irrelevant. It is perhaps possible to find a starting point for our analysis, if we suppose the authorities to continue to behave in the same way as they were behaving in the preceding period of full employ-

L

ment.   Suppose a turn in the circumstances to occur,
such as a fall in world prices, which, if the exchanges
were held stable, would entail a loss of income at home.
Suppose that the process of falling income is already
beginning.   Suppose further that individuals, corporate
bodies, etc., show on balance a sublime indifference to
this loss of income and continue to spend as much as
before.   The foreign exchange rate will at once move
downwards and the production of A and B output will be
restimulated.   If consumers generally are absolutely
resolute in maintaining expenditure, the foreign exchange
rates will be so depressed that the A and B output and
the level of incomes will be maintained at their old level.
The bold policy of maintaining expenditure will lead to
the result that no reduction of expenditure will ultimately
prove necessary ; for incomes will be sustained.

If on the other hand consumers reduce expenditure in
proportion to the initial loss of income, the reduction of
income will proceed ; and, if the reduction of expenditure
is always kept in line with the reduction of income, there
will be no depression in the exchange rate at all, and
precisely the same volume of unemployment will ensue
as if the country had been on the gold standard.   No
advantage will have been taken of the newly found freedom.   Such a consequence would not be unnatural.
Individuals may well think it right and proper to balance
their private budgets.   The net effect of the adverse
turn may be intermediate between the two extremes
here mentioned.   Individuals may show some propensity
to spend more than their incomes without going to the
extreme of maintaining their old expenditure.   In this
case the result will not be so bad as that under gold
standard conditions, but it will not be so satisfactory

as what is possible. The fall in sterling prices will not be so severe as that under the gold standard, but there will be some fall.

Two courses are open to the authorities if they wish to maintain the value of the currency (in terms of world commodities) stable. They may operate directly on the exchanges and depress them sufficiently to prevent an excessive fall of A and B output and to maintain the previous level of general incomes[1]; or they may operate directly on incomes, sustaining them at their old level, and so cause a depression of the exchanges indirectly. This second policy also involves countering any hoarding which may occur by raising incomes above their old level so as to maintain expenditure at its old level. The final result of these two policies should in principle be the same. It should be observed that if the authorities get off the mark sufficiently quickly the operations need not be on a large scale. If they make good the initial loss of income, which is small, the consequent fall in the exchanges will prevent that loss getting larger.

The process of operating on the exchanges is a simpler one than supplementing incomes. In the former case the authorities merely buy foreign exchange, in the latter they do—what? If the upshot is the same, they should surely choose the simpler process! That conclusion is valid if they do act quickly. But if they miss the golden opportunity and wait for the depression to gather force, *other considerations* arise. Nor, human knowledge and

[1] Since in these circumstances h will probably fall (cf. p. 114), the value of A and B output expressed in home currency may drop somewhat, while general income is maintained at its old level.

human will being what they are, can we expect them to act with absolute promptitude. The discussions in the seven sub-sections above should have sufficed to show that there may be difficulties in interpreting the situation aright. The maladjustment may have to become rather crude before they can see what it is correctly and take appropriate action.

What are the "other considerations" if the gap between the ideal and the actual has become rather large ? *The effects of the country's action on the external world.* These may not matter very much if the country is fairly small and the rest of the world fairly prosperous. But, if the country bulks large in the world economy and if a severe world slump is in process, these effects may be important ; they will be more important the larger the gap which has been allowed to appear. It may be inferred that they are as important as they well can be at the present time when a gigantic reflation is called for, when the country is as great as England and when the outer world is suffering from an unprecedented slump.

The difference between the external effects of the two methods is easy to see. In one case the outer world is confronted with a persistent and relentless offer of cheap supplies by the reflationary country, unaccompanied by a proportionate increase in her demand. The gap between her supply and her demand will be precisely equal to the amount of foreign exchange that the authorities have to purchase in order to get the rate sufficiently low. (To this must be added any adverse speculative movement of funds from the reflating country, which may be caused by her exchange depreciation.) This devastating fire of cheap goods will further weaken the world price level, and this will increase the exchange depreciation which the reflating country has to bring about in order to secure reflation. The difficulties of the outer world will be *pro tanto* aggravated ; the aggravation of a disease, when the situation is already desperate, is apt to have effects out of proportion to the size of the cause.

The other line of action has very different effects. If the incomes of the reflating country are raised by the action of the authorities, the first impact on the outer world will be an increased *demand* for world goods. This, it is true, will be followed by a fall in the deflating country's exchange rates and an increasing offer by her of cheap goods. But her increment of supply will at no time exceed her increment of demand and there will be no depressing effect on the general world price level. (There will, of course, be shifts between particular commodities.) Now that the authorities are no longer trying to force the exchange down, they may properly counter any adverse speculative movement by the use of their available reserves. In the case of a big reflation they would do well to mobilize a large reserve of foreign assets, not with the idea that they would be ultimately lost, but as a fighting fund against alarmist withdrawals. If the fighting fund were of ample size, the malign effects of alarmists would be frustrated and their money would automatically come back. If any thought is to be given to the external world, the decision must be in favour of the second method of reflation. If the external world is in extreme jeopardy, thought must be given to its interests; no reflation, however firm, will avail against the repercussions on the reflating country which would be caused by a complete external breakdown.

If the reflating country was in a really benevolent

mood, she would actually hold her exchange rates above the level naturally determined by the increase of her internal income, selling foreign assets in order to do so. (This level would, however, be much lower than that which would rule in the absence of reflation). Such a policy would make the country's increment of demand exceed her increment of supply, and tend to lift the world price level.

It remains to consider how the authorities can raise the level of internal incomes. The traditional method is to encourage capital construction by means of low interest rates. This, if effective, raises the volume of C industry incomes, and in consequence the expenditure on all classes of goods.

The traditional method is not likely to be effective in a time of deep depression. For one thing, when production is at a low level, and much plant is lying idle, the demand for new plant is not likely to be strong, however low the rate at which money can be borrowed. Furthermore the demand for new capital depends on its prospective yield ; and, if there is no guarantee that its future yield will not fall in value and volume, a low rate of interest is not likely to encourage its construction. The authorities may say : " We are embarking on a policy of reflation ; have no fear that prices and turnover will fall further ; on the contrary they will rise." To which the appropriate answer is : " How can you guarantee that prices will not fall ? How is your reflation to be brought about ? " The authorities may then say : " We intend to maintain interest rates at a low level," and be answered, " Interest rates have been at a low level for the last year, and prices have continued to fall." This is an adequate reply to the authorities ; if the depression is deep the mere maintenance of low interest rates is unlikely to bring about a speedy revival.

What other means have the authorities at their disposal to increase internal incomes? Many. The central government and local authorities take away from the citizens annually vast sums of money, most of which they spend, some of which they use to pay off debt. Internal incomes could be increased if these authorities took in taxation less money than they paid away and found the difference by borrowing. The ordinary method of banking expansion breaks down in a depression because the banks cannot find sound new borrowers. Let the government be that new borrower. How much of the loans the government should use to finance new public works and how much to remit taxation depends on the particular circumstances of the case.

This is a safe and certain means of raising internal incomes and so causing the foreign exchange rates to settle at a high output level, without inflicting any injury on the outer world. It may even be arranged to have a stimulating effect outside. If one or two strong countries deliberately engaged in policy of this sort, a world revival might be considerably hastened. If a large number of countries agreed to act simultaneously, that would be still better, but they are not likely to commit themselves to a monetary policy affecting their national budgets, until sound economic doctrine on these subjects is much more widely diffused than at present.

It might be objected to this policy that the interest on the government borrowing involves a fresh burden on the community in future. The reasonings of this chapter have indicated that on balance in the long period the occasions on which the authorities should act in the sense of raising the exchange rates are likely to be at least as numerous as those in which they should do the opposite. On the former occasions a strong sinking fund policy is called for, and the interest burden of the government debt would be relieved accordingly. Furthermore, the interest burden involved by reflationary borrowing is microscopic compared with the loss of income due to a severe depression.

Whether the future course of events is likely to call for the continued use of the government borrowing and sinking fund method to secure monetary stability depends on how far world monetary reform is achieved. If world monetary fluctuations are confined within narrow limits the traditional banking methods of expansion and contraction may well suffice. But, in view of the dense cloud of ignorance which enshrouds the monetary authorities in most countries, it would be rash to be too optimistic about world reform. It is important that a country, such as England, which by reason of its unitary financial system and great traditions is singularly well place to give a lead in these matters, should accustom its mind to the new technique. Other financial considerations which might influence the government in deciding whether to borrow or have a strong sinking fund are but straws in the balance compared with the importance of securing monetary stability.

CHAPTER VIII

WORLD MONETARY REFORM

§ 1. *The Trade Cycle*. The subject of the last chapter naturally leads on to a survey of the world monetary system. The world in this context must not be taken too literally. Not all parts of the world are as closely linked together as some. The world monetary system may be thgouht of as all embracing, but some sections of the system are slower to feel the effects of general influences and less effective in reacting on the other sections; this may be due to their geographical remoteness, to the primitive nature of their economic life or to their having, like Soviet Russia, deliberately cut themselves out of the system in some measure.

With the exception of China the whole system has in recent years maintained or endeavoured in normal times to maintain a gold standard. All the countries which have done this have had in a very real sense a common money. Units of money of the same denomination are interchangeable with one another inside each country; the units of money of the different countries adhering to the gold standard are also within very narrow limits of fluctuation interchangeable with units of others according to the gold valuation of each. The total quantity of money in the system is equal to the total amount of gold set aside for use as money plus the total amount of the loans of all the banks. (To this must be added any outstanding fiduciary note issues of governments.)

As far as the eye of the economic historian can see back into the past at all clearly, production and trade in the various countries have been subject to a general fluctuation, affecting most branches of business, commonly known as the Trade Cycle. In recent times this has tended to become a world phenomenon, in the sense that its phases have tended to occur at the same time in all the closely linked countries.

After the war it was hoped that the amplitude of the fluctuation might be reduced, especially as the new central banking system in the (economically) largest country, the U.S.A., was explicitly committed to an attempt to reduce this amplitude through the monetary machinery at its disposal. The hope has not been fulfilled. The depression of 1933 represents a recession from the previous level of output and trade greater than any that previously occurred in recorded history. This tidal movement, if we may so regard it, has now become so great that there is a possibility, some think, of its shattering the world of capitalist organization in which it is taking place.

Of the causes of this movement little is known, though of the interaction of forces which occur when the movement manifests itself something is understood. Any attempt to summarize the theories of the subject which have been put forward would be too bulky for insertion in this book. An outline may be given of the monetary conditions that would be the prerequisite of a steady advance.

It may be laid down that the increase in the flow of monetary demand in the world should, in some sense, keep pace with the increased capacity for producing goods. It is proper to assume at the present time an increasing population in the system and an increase of potential output per head. In what precise sense the increase of money should keep pace it is our immediate task to enquire. Failing such conformity there would be now a general rise, now a fall, in the value of money. There are two special points in this connection. It is known from historical survey that the fluctuations in general economic activity have in fact been associated with changes in the value of money, advances generally with a fall and recessions with a rise. Secondly, when changes in the value of money occur, all prices do not move equally. The prices of the various valuables are of course always shifting relatively to each other. But the shifts in the price of big classes of valuables relatively to each other, which are associated with the trade cycle, seem to be due to, or aspects of, changes in the value of money itself. These shifts may be explained by the fact that the markets for some valuables, e.g. A goods, are organized much more perfectly to make prices respond to changes in monetary demand than those for others, e.g. labour. It seems reasonable therefore to suppose that the changes in the value of money are not unconnected with the disturbances of the trade cycle and that it would be desirable to provide a measure of value, the value of which was not itself liable to violent fluctuation.

Stability may be achieved in two ways, by each country cutting itself off from the rest of the world and maintaining an autonomous standard, or by international co-operation. Stability without international co-operation must be at best partial. Such a method presupposes fluctuations in the foreign exchange rates of the stabilized currency, which, if other monetary systems are badly mismanaged, will be large.

If output per head is rising, the average price of factors must be rising relatively to the average price of goods. From this it follows that however we define absolute steadiness in the value of money there is certainly unsteadiness if the average price of factors is falling or the average price of goods rising. In other words, there is unsteadiness if the average price of goods falls more than the average increase in output per head or if the average price of factors rises by more than that increase.

§ 2.   *The Maintenance of Monetary Demand.* It is desirable that the monetary demand for goods in the world should rise not less than the increase of factors of production and not more than the increased quantity of goods capable of being produced. The monetary demand for goods can only increase if one of two things happens. Either individuals must on balance continually raise the rate of their expenditure in relation to their income, i.e. turn their money over more and more quickly, or a continual stream of fresh money must be injected into the system.

Changes in the rate of turnover do in fact occur. There are ups and downs in the short period associated with the trade cycle. These should be offset by altering proportionately the stream of fresh money coming into the system and even, if necessary, taking money out of the system. It is not claimed that such compensatory action would eliminate the trade cycle; it could be used to eliminate changes in the value of money associated with the cycle; if it is true, as seems highly probable, that those monetary changes aggravate the cycle, the amplitude of the cycle would be *pro tanto* diminished ; the scale of compensatory action required would be less, the more promptly and effectively the action was carried out.

Velocity of turnover may change in the long period also. There is probably some tendency towards an increase in countries where the use of banking accounts is being substituted for cash. This increase, when it occurs, reduces the size of the stream of fresh money that is required to maintain monetary demand.

If the gold standard is in use, some of the fresh money may take the form of newly mined gold. But, as the money consisting of or backed by gold is small compared with the total amount of money in use, this source of new supply is unlikely to be adequate. If the stock of monetary gold were rising at the rate of 2 per cent per annum this would only mean an increase in the quantity of money of a small fraction of 1 per cent per annum. The stream of new gold will need to be supplemented by the other source of new money, bank lendings. When a bank makes additional loans, the incomes of the factors paid with this money constitute a net addition to total pre-existing incomes and consequently to the monetary demand for goods.

If the banks always observed the supposed " pre-war rules of the gold standard,"[1] and maintained a constant ratio between bank loans and gold reserves, the rate at which the total stock of money increased would be the same as that at which the monetary gold stock increased. If this system were adopted, it would be inadequate for two reasons. (i) It would do nothing to offset periodic changes in the velocity of turnover. (ii) The rate of

[1] Ch. V, p. 98.

increase in monetary gold might be insufficient to provide a sufficient rate of increase in monetary demand, or it might be excessive. There is reason to believe that in future it will prove insufficient.[1] Nor does it appear that the " pre-war rules " have ever been widely adopted or are consistent with banking traditions. Their supposed prevalence cannot be reconciled with the fluctuations in the total quantity of money in different countries which have in fact occurred. In times of depression the banks may be unable to find sound new borrowers, and the expedient of government borrowing from the banks at such times is a comparatively recent maxim—and is not yet officially recognized.

The means by which the monetary authorities may increase or diminish the streams of monetary demand, namely by alterations in the banks' terms of lending and by alterations in the government's policy of borrowing and debt redemption, have already been discussed in the last chapter. World monetary reform is not likely to be successful until the possibility and necessity of governmental assistance in the process is widely understood.

§ 3. *Alternative Projects*. In discussing the details of world reform, are we to assume that the gold standard is retained or abandoned ? There are six possibilities. (i) An unreformed world gold standard. (ii) An unreformed world money, without a gold par, but with fixed exchanges between countries. (iii) An unreformed system, without gold and without fixed exchanges between countries (some of which may remain on gold). (iv) A reformed world gold standard. (v) A reformed world

[1] Cf. *The International Gold Problem*, publication of the Royal Institute of International Affairs, pp. 47–48.

money, without a gold par, but with fixed exchanges between countries. (vi) A reformed world system, without a gold par and without fixed exchanges between countries, the rates being made to move in accordance with the principles of the system. (To these may be added a seventh, a reformed world gold standard but with adjustments in the gold content of national currencies [cf. Prof. Irving Fisher's plan[1]] and corresponding movements in the rates of exchange between currencies in accordance with the principles of the system. This seventh alternative bears the same relation to the fourth as the sixth does to the fifth.) Of the possibilities, the first three, excluding world reform but not necessarily excluding reform in particular countries, do not belong to this discussion. The word "reform" rather than "management" is used in this context advisedly. All six alternatives, with the possible exception of the third in certain circumstances, involve management of the currencies. Reform means management with the specific object of stabilizing their value. Of the remaining three, the choice between the fourth and fifth is of secondary importance except to gold-mining interests and goldsmiths. If the world decides to co-operate in order to secure a common money, stable in terms of commodities, it does not much matter whether the unit has a constant value in terms of gold or not. The same methods would be required to achieve stability and the same results would flow from it. If the gold standard were adopted, the system would have the incidental effect of regulating the value of gold. This would of course be important for gold interests, but it would be a matter of indifference to every one else.

[1] Professor Irving Fisher, *Purchasing Power of Money*, ch. 13.

The really important choice is between the fifth (which
we may take as roughly equivalent to the fourth) and the
sixth, and it is to the considerations affecting the choice
between them that we must now address ourselves. If
it were decided to adopt the sixth, but it was still desired
to make some use of gold, for sentimental reasons, to
please the public, or to pacify gold interests, then the
seventh alternative, a variant of the sixth involving the
use of gold, could be adopted.

The object in choosing the sixth rather than the fifth
would be to secure an adaptation of the system to special
national interests. But it must not be supposed that this
involves an abandonment of world reform and a reversion
to the plan of each nation controlling the value of its
money independently. National reform undertaken in a
world co-operating in the endeavour to secure stability
in money generally is a very different thing from national
reform undertaken in an unreformed world. The former
could be carried out much more easily and would be
certain to achieve better results.

§ 4. *Plan for a Common Stable World Money.* Three
variations on the fifth theme will first be considered.

(i) The simplest project for world reform would be to
aim at the stability of money in terms of A commodities.
These have common world prices which can easily be
ascertained. The object would be to keep the general
index of A prices stationary. Absolute stability could
not be guaranteed; a fluctuation of 2 or 3 or even 5 per
cent around a given par would have to be allowed, but
such movements must not be cumulative.

This would be the easiest of all projects for which to
secure agreement, if indeed it is appropriate to use the

word easy at all in such a context, for agreement could only be secured with extreme difficulty. The system, though far better than anything for which we may hope in an unreformed world, would be open to serious objections. There is reason to believe that the A goods price level will be subject to a long-period downward trend, relatively to other prices.[1] Stabilization of the A price level would then involve a rising level of general prices and would carry us outside the limits for stability already laid down.[2] It would be slightly inflationary. It would also affect different countries differently. The inflation would be greatest in countries specializing in B output, and in those having a large proportion of C output. Inflation is not necessarily an evil, provided that it is gradual and steady, as it would be under the system ; but inflation is apt to get out of hand, and the smooth working of the world system would necessitate every country keeping a proper control over its own conditions. The whole scheme might be jeopardized if inflation got out of hand in a particular country. The dangers of even a moderate degree of inflation are likely to be accentuated if stock exchange speculation is a widespread practice ; and the interest of the mass of people in this activity will probably grow apace in coming years.

(ii) An alternative would be to stablize world money in terms of A and B and even C goods. This would be a much more cumbersome affair, as it would be necessary to get sample quotations of B and C commodities from all countries. The prices of these differ from country to country. The world index must include numerous quotations for each of these commodities weighted

[1] Cf. ch. III, pp. 52–54.
[2] Cf. p. 162.

M

according to the size and importance of the area for which each quotation is valid. This plan would eliminate the inflationary element from the system, but is open to two objections of its own, besides the obvious practical difficulty of compiling an accurate world index. Both objections are of fundamental importance in principle.

The first is that the inclusion of the vast mass of B and C commodities, weighted according to their importance in relation to the A group, might render the world index too little sensitive to changes in monetary conditions. The object of the whole scheme of reform is to secure that monetary demand should rise sufficiently to give full employment to the available productive resources. If demand falls, or fails to increase sufficiently, this is reflected in a fall of A prices. The fall in B and C prices is often far smaller or does not occur at all. When this happens it must not be inferred that there has been a shift in the demand between these classes of goods or that there was previously a relative over-production of A goods.[1] B and C prices fail to fall for two reasons. In the first instance their prices are sustained because producers are better placed to curtail output drastically, either because they are monopolistic, or because they have that quasi-monopolistic nature, which direct contact with customers, unmediated by an organized market, gives. Secondly, these goods are less likely to be subject to increasing costs, for the range of output below the pre-existent level, i.e. costs will not fall as output is curtailed, and the producers will be bound in their own

[1] In discussions of the crisis of 1929–1933 the importance attached to this relative over-production, which may indeed have been present in a moderate degree (Cf. ch. III, pp. 52–54) has been grossly exaggerated.

interest to curtail output sufficiently to maintain prices near their old level.[1] The failure of these prices to fall does not mean that the monetary demand for the commodities has not fallen, but only that supply has been more drastically restricted. Consequently the presence of these unresponsive prices in the index number will tend to mask what is really happening in the monetary system. If such an index number were taken as their sole guide by the monetary authorities, the maintenance of an appropriate flow of purchasing power might not be achieved.

A distinction, however, must be drawn between the policy and the criteria used to facilitate the policy. The policy here under examination is to secure such a flow of purchasing power that, when fundamental conditions of demand and cost tended to make A prices move downwards relative to the others, the A prices should not be sustained at a stable level, but should move downward somewhat while other prices moved upward somewhat, so that the general level remained stable. Yet movements in this general index may fail to be an adequate criterion for the direction of the policy. This criterion might be supplemented by others, such as the volume of output in B and C industries or the volume of employment. Thus, if A prices moved downwards, but output and employment in other industries was sustained at a full level, no addition to the stream of money would be called for. But, if A prices moved downwards *and* unemployment began to appear in the other industries, then, even if B and C prices remained stationary or rose, an expansion of money would be required. In other words the policy of stabilizing the monetary demand for all goods (as

[1] Cf. ch. IV, p. 67.

opposed to that for A goods only) should be secured not by adverting to an index of general prices, but to an index of A prices combined with B and C production, turnover or employment indices.

The second fundamental objection to the project before us is that it would work unevenly for different countries. The relative shift between C prices and A prices may be different from place to place. In rapidly advancing communities C prices tend to rise relatively to A prices with proportional rapidity,[1] while in stationary communities there may be no shift. The scheme would then produce a condition of rising general prices in the former and falling general prices in the latter class of countries. The less progressive countries would thus be afflicted with the additional inconvenience of a deflatory monetary system. Inflation would occur just where it is most dangerous, namely, in the rapidly advancing countries. This objection appears in one form or another in all projects for a common world money, and will be brought out more clearly in the next proposal we have to consider.

(iii) Ricardo held that a perfect measure of value should always purchase commodities containing the same amount of labour. This view has found more recent advocates. It would involve a constant average price of factors of production, with commodity prices falling at the rate that efficiency increased. Any attempt to introduce such a standard would be beset with the same difficulties, but in a more intense form, that would stand in the way of a stable general commodity price level.

In the first place a world index of wages, salaries, rents, etc., containing sample quotations from every country, could be constructed, but it would be absolutely useless as

[1] Cf. ch. IV, sec. 4.

a criterion for giving effect to the policy. These rewards do not respond readily to changes in demand for services ; monetary demand might fall right away and widespread unemployment ensue without any change in the index number occurring at all. Thus, if the authorities were using this index number as a guide, they would have no clue that an increase of money was required. Nor would the criterion reflect the effect of changes in their policy. They might inject new money or withdraw money in use and thus produce big changes in monetary demand, while the general index of wages, etc., remained constant all the time. Thus our first objection to the use of a general commodity price index comes out in the proposal to use a general factor price index in a much more striking form.

It might be suggested that the authorities should frame some estimate of the rate at which factors (working population, etc.) were increasing, and secure that monetary demand increased at that rate. This would solve the long-period problem, but it would do nothing to offset short-period changes in monetary demand due to changes in the rate of hoarding and dis-hoarding by people generally. It would do nothing to solve the trade cycle problem ; it would probably have done little to avert the present monetary chaos.

An alternative method of securing guidance, but a very different one, might be to frame some estimate of the rate at which average efficiency was increasing. The authorities would then decide to make the general commodity price level fall at this rate. They would use the commodity price level as their indicator for action, but, instead of stabilizing that, they would make it fall at the rate of 1 per cent per annum, or whatever was the

estimated increase of efficiency.   They would still have
the problem of the unsatisfactory character of the general
commodity price index.   If they also attempted to estimate
the normal rate of shift between A and other prices and
used the A index as their criterion, they would at least
have a sensitive criterion, but both their estimates would
probably be of a very arbitrary character.

The efficiency of countries increases at different rates.
If the general commodity prices fell at a rate equal to the
average increase in world efficiency, the comparatively
stationary countries would have to make their rewards
to factors fall progressively.   This would be highly
inconvenient.   The measure of stability secured for them
would fall outside the limits set down above for a stable
monetary system.   Their position would be intolerable
and it would be difficult to secure their agreement to such
a policy.

The three specific projects for reform considered in
this section are all variations on the fifth (or fourth) main
theme.   What emerges seems to be this.   The first
variant is simple and manageable and would be an
immense improvement on present conditions.   Its danger
is that it contains an inflationary element.   If agreement
could be secured for it, an experiment would be worth
while.   The practical difficulties of securing satisfactory
criteria for the second and third variants and the different
incidence on countries advancing in productive efficiency
at different rates, which they necessarily involve, suggest
that it would be worth turning our attention to the sixth
theme.

§ 5.   *Plan for a Stable World Money with National
Variations*.   The essence of this is that world reform

might be undertaken through international co-operation without its necessarily involving a common world money. The divergence of the interests of different countries could be recognized and allowed for. The rates at which their respective currencies exchange against each other would be made to change in a regular and orderly manner.

It might be objected at the outset that stability of exchange is a great convenience, obtainable even under the bad old regime, and that monetary reform that did not secure it would hardly be worth having. Broadly, however, stability of exchange would be secured. Changes in the rates envisaged would never be likely to exceed 2 per cent in the course of the year and would probably not be so great. If the changes are to be as small as this, why should they not be dispensed with altogether? The answer is that these changes, unlike ordinary fluctuations, would usually be all in the same direction; while causing little inconvenience to the ordinary conduct of business, their cumulative effect on the economic situation would be large. Ten years soon pass. Corrective changes in the foreign exchange rates of 2 per cent per annum amount to 22 per cent in ten years. A maladjustment of 22 per cent between home rewards and world prices, which would presumably be outstanding at the end of ten years, if the correction were not applied, is a major disaster. The changes would be applied by the national authorities, in accordance with the world plan for monetary reform, and in agreement with the other countries; and, in the intervals between the changes, the exchange would be held within fixed limits of par as under the ordinary gold standard.

The object of the scheme is to secure stability of value for each separate currency as well as general stability.

In the case of the national situation, as in that of the world situation, three variations on the theme of stability may be imagined : stability of the A price level, stability of the general price level, and a general price level falling in proportion to the rise of average efficiency. If the first variant is preferred, then there is no need for separate national monies ; A prices are world prices ; if the British A price level is stable, so will the French and German price levels be too ; each and every country can secure a stable price level in this sense and have stable rates of exchange between them.

But, if each nation seeks to have stability for itself in the second or third senses, there can be no common world standard. The currencies of the more progressive countries must be made to appreciate in terms of the others. Suppose that the third variant is preferred, and efficiency in country X is advancing at 2 per cent per annum, while that in Y at 1 per cent only ; prices should fall 2 per cent in X and only 1 per cent in Y ; if there is no change in the relation between A prices and B and C prices in either country, A prices must fall 2 per cent in X and only 1 per cent in Y. Consequently the money of X must rise 1 per cent in terms of that of Y. If, owing to the changes in efficiency, all goods rise 1 per cent in X relatively to A goods and only $\frac{1}{2}$ per cent in Y, and it is required that general prices should fall 2 per cent in X and 1 per cent in Y, the money of X must rise $1\frac{1}{2}$ per cent in terms of that of Y. If the second variant is preferred and stability in the general prices is sought, the X currency need in these circumstances only rise $\frac{1}{2}$ per cent in terms of Y. Such adjustments might hastily be dismissed as piffling. To do so would be quite erroneous, since, if they are all in the same direction, as they may be expected to be, their cumulative effect will be large.

The scheme is that world stability should be secured by international co-operation, while each nation should decide on the basis of her own conditions whether she desired the A price level, expressed in her own currency, to remain stable or to fall by 1 per cent or 2 per cent per annum, or whatever the amount might be. In deciding this she must take account of matters already discussed (in Ch. VII, Sec. 2), namely, the rate at which efficiency is rising compared with the rate at which she may find it convenient on balance to raise rewards to factors, the long-period trend of h, the long-period trend of the non-trading items in her balance-sheet, etc. No doubt she may have some perplexity in reaching a decision. But her perplexities would be much less than those of a world committee endeavouring to decide how it wished to make the world A level behave, for it would have to deal in magnitudes, consisting of averages covering conflicting tendencies in different countries.

Each country would communicate to the international committee how much it wanted its A price level to fall. There should probably be some maximum such as 2 per cent per annum outside which a country would not be allowed to opt. The committee could then readily compute what the official course of all the foreign exchanges would be. The changes in the official pars of exchange might well be spread; for instance, the dollar—sterling official rate might fall by $\frac{1}{100}$ of a cent a day, so that the change in the par in the course of ninety days would still be much smaller than the possible fluctuations (due to market conditions) about the par.

Decisions of particular countries should not be

irrevocable; they should on the contrary be subject to frequent revision. It must be stressed that the data on which such decisions are based are all computed by long-period trends and have nothing whatever to do with trade cycle or other short-period phenomena. We are here concerned only with whether it is desirable that *in the long run* a country's A price level should be stable or decline gently.

So far no account has been taken of tariff changes. It is clear that these have an intimate connection with monetary arrangements. A country deciding to raise the general level of her import duties, or to impose an important set of additional duties, would have to make up her mind whether this was intended to be a precursor to a domestic inflation or not. In the former case no change in her exchange rates need occur. Her total volume of imports would not be reduced; but the representative man would spend a smaller fraction of his income on imports and their specific content might change.[1] It must be clear, however, that an inflation of more than moderate dimensions would jeopardize the whole international system—for instance, by causing big special movements of capital to the stock market of the inflating country—and would be entirely contrary to the spirit, if not to the letter, if there be a letter, of the agreement. If she wishes to avoid an internal inflation, her rate of foreign exchange must be raised sufficiently to offset the effects of the tariff. The special interests favoured by the tariff might not relish this plan; since, however, the change in the rate of exchange would affect all A and B producers while the tariff only affected some, the percentage change in the rate would not be as high

[1] For a further explanation of this, see ch. IX, sec. 4, p. 199.

as the tariff ; thus the protected producers would gain on balance and all other producers would demonstrably lose ; the protected producers could still have grounds for rejoicing, while others suffered ; the true inward nature of a tariff would thus be plainly exposed to the general view, and the public would at last have materials to judge for itself on the desirability of tariff-making. The fact is, this problem brings into direct juxtaposition the old primitive and barbarous ideas of economics belonging to the past, on which tariff-making is based, and the new scientific ideas of the future. The two simply will not mix.

§ 6. *Giving Effect to the Plan.* So far this chapter has been concerned with objectives and, to some extent, with criteria for determining policy calculated to achieve them. Little has been said about how this policy is to be carried out. It is well to take stock of the present position. The alternative objectives considered amount to : (i) a stable level of A prices ; (ii) a level of A prices gradually falling everywhere ; (iii) a level of A prices gradually falling everywhere but at a slightly different rate in each country with consequential adjustments in the exchange value of their currencies. Under any of these plans the monetary authorities of each country would be responsible for maintaining their official pars of exchange, precisely as they are responsible under the unreformed gold standard. But this would not be the end of their responsibility. The maintenance of exchange rates is compatible with a world inflation and a world deflation, and the aim is to avoid either of these. Along with the responsibility of maintaining her exchange, each nation would share the responsibility for maintaining stability in the world monetary system ; to do this each nation must contribute her part to the new stream of monetary demand required to maintain stability, or, if a tendency towards private dishoarding appeared, must contribute her part towards thinning out the existing stream of monetary demand. This is the essence and meaning of international co-operation.

This end could be secured in one of two ways. Either each country could receive and follow the guidance of an international committee and increase or diminish her stream of new money accordingly, or the central bank of each country could agree to hold part of its reserves at an international bank which would be able to regulate the world stream of new money, by open market operations in every country. It cannot be denied that the working of this system would be beset with serious difficulties.

The monetary system when left to itself seems to be subject to an inherent instability. The object of reform is to counteract this tendency by varying the rate of monetary expansion from time to time. At first sight it might seem that some sort of quota system would be appropriate, each country undertaking normally to expand her circulating medium by an agreed amount proportional to her size and importance in the world economy. The central committee or bank could then apply to each quota a coefficient appropriate to the existing phase of world business. It might thus instruct each country to double, quadruple, or halve her normal rate of expansion, according to whether mild deflationary, strong deflationary, or inflationary world conditions were tending to come into existence and needed offsetting. This solution is unfortunately too simple. Tendencies to hoarding or dishoarding may appear with very different force in different countries ; doubling the normal expansion of money in circulation might be accompanied by a doubling of monetary demand in one and by a falling off of monetary demand in another. It is the duty of each country so to regulate its monetary system that its effective monetary demand expands by an appropriate amount. It does not seem possible to lay down any rule of thumb governing this regulation. It is doubtful if the central committee could do more than issue such orders as " expand more quickly," " expand much more quickly," " stop expansion," or " contract." Or, if there was an international bank, it could provide the different countries with such increase of cash basis as it thought appropriate, trusting that they would expand credit in proportion.

These are difficulties, however, which it is useless to attempt to solve on paper. They can only be solved by experience. What is essential is that the countries which adhere to the arrangement should understand the objective clearly and wish its fulfilment. The root difficulty is that, whether it is a rise or fall of prices that has to be checked, the authorities have to act in a way that is against the grain. They have to be repeatedly setting themselves against the pyschological impulses of the mob. Furthermore, in a time of depression those who were disloyal to the system would seem to gain thereby ; those who failed to expand as quickly as others would have an active balance of payments ; the virtuous would be punished for their virtue, unless all were virtuous. That is always so in a time of deflation ; the cowardly and selfish are rewarded. For the system to work, therefore, it is essential that all should be loyal to it.

It would also be essential for the success of the system, that all countries should be able as well as willing to increase monetary demand by the appropriate amount. It would be no excuse for one country to say : " But we have kept interest rates as low as we can, and the monetary demand simply has not increased." Every government must be prepared to take action to assist the banks, if necessary, and increase their borrowings when an increase of money is called for, or repay debt when a reduction is called for. Until this maxim is recognized, with all the goodwill in the world, international co-operation will probably be impotent to achieve its objective.

In the last chapter it was seen that a particular country, resolutely determined to stabilize her money, might do much to maintain her productive resources in full use. But the repercussions of severe instability in the outer world might prove too strong for her. This external instability is apt to produce large and sudden movements in the non-trading items on her foreign balance-sheet, and the repercussions due to these are difficult to offset and perhaps ought not to be offset by currency policy. The position of a country depending mainly on B output is difficult to secure if her foreign markets shrivel up. It is the duty therefore of every country which desires that her productive resources should be adequately employed both to carry out monetary reform herself and to press for international reform.

That general acceptance could be secured for reform of the kind suggested here or for any valuable scheme of reform in the near future is not even remotely probable. Indeed the whole of this piece of analysis might be condemned as merely academic. But times change. The application of scientific knowledge to the technique of production advanced rapidly in the days of the industrial revolution, and might have surprised an earlier generation. So it may happen that scientific ideas will ultimately come to be applied in the economic sphere. It is the duty of economists to give them body and cogency. The present generation of politicians and bankers will pass away. They will endeavour to hand on their stock of meaningless clichés to those who succeed them. But even clichés pass out of fashon in time. The present generation might be surprised if they could see what the future will bring.

CHAPTER IX

TARIFFS

§ 1. *Origins*. The evolution of a workable system of currency has been a slow and laborious process. Between the fall of the Roman Empire and the thirteenth century silver was the sole standard in Europe. The growing bulk of commerce led to the introduction of gold by the Italian cities in the thirteenth century and by France and England in the fourteenth. The system of bimetallism was adopted. But it was not worked satisfactorily. The need for different countries to have the same mint ratio between gold and silver was not appreciated, and ratios seldom were the same. Consequently each country was subjected to a loss of gold or silver. This was met on the one hand by stringent but ineffective prohibitions against the export of the precious metals and on the other by the progressive debasement of the standard. It was found by experiment that the debasement of coins containing the disappearing metal checked the outflow; for the debasement made the ratio more favourable to this metal. But it was often carried too far, the other metal began to disappear and the coins embodying it had to be debased in their turn.

An enlightened school of thought arose in England in the seventeenth century, which condemned the laws against exportation, on the ground that they were ineffective and that, by presenting an obstacle to those who wished to use the country as an entrepôt, they reduced the profits arising from foreign trade, and so checked the inflow of metals which would result therefrom.

The prohibitions were abolished in 1663. To prevent the disturbances which were still liable to result from discrepancies between the bimetallic ratios, gold was for the time demonetized in England. Golden guineas were coined but allowed to circulate at their market value.

That the prohibitions were originally introduced in the Middle Ages to meet practical exigencies was forgotten. Meanwhile Spain had endeavoured to enforce prohibitions from another motive; having laid her hand on great sources of output of the precious metals in the new world, she thought that the resulting flow of wealth would be frittered away if the metals were allowed to leave the country. Wealth was identified with the possession of large stocks of precious metals.

Mun and his school, who recommended the repeal of the prohibitions, did not repudiate the notion, which had thus gained currency, that it was the proper object of the prohibitions to secure for the country a greatest possible stock of precious metals. The object was still thought to be a sound one; the means were discarded as unsuitable. Some more scientific means must be found. If it could be secured that the country always had a favourable balance of trade in commodities, the excess of exports would be paid for in gold and there would be a permanent inflow. To secure a favourable balance, an excellent weapon was to hand, the customs duties. These had hitherto been mainly regarded as a source of revenue. Now, it was laid down, they must be carefully manipulated so as to maintain a favourable balance of trade.

N

This was the prevalent theory for a hundred years. Adam Smith's attack on it had two parts. He set out to show first that an accumulation of precious metals was not a proper object of policy, and secondly that the import duties did not secure a permanent favourable balance of trade. Both lines of criticism were effective and final.

Meanwhile tariffs had come to be favoured in Europe as means of fostering native industries. Against this view Adam Smith argued that capital would, if unimpeded, find its way into those occupations for which the country was most suited.[1] With the passage of time there has been a further development of protectionist doctrines ; an attempt is made in the following pages to assess the validity of those which have been supported by serious argument.

§ 2. *Two Special Arguments*. (i) *Self-sufficiency*. (ii) *Bargaining*. In the first place two arguments may be referred to which are of a rather special kind.

(i) It may be desired to forego the economic advantages flowing from the international division of labour in the interest of making a country self-sufficient either in all respects or in respect of certain commodities supposed to be of vital importance in time of war. The nature of this argument is plain, and its importance the reader can estimate for himself. It is clear that the desire for self-sufficiency, if pressed to its logical conclusion, would entail the sacrifice of all the gain accruing from the international division of labour and lead to a very great

[1] It was in defining this view more sharply that Ricardo enunciated the principle of comparative costs. (See chapter II, sec. 3).

impoverishment in all countries. Unhappily the tendency in this direction has never been so strong as it is at present.

(ii) The imposition of a tariff to induce other countries to lower theirs was admitted as a legitimate exception to Free Trade policy even by Adam Smith. This argument is consistent with the view that both foreign tariffs and tariffs imposed by the home country are injurious to the home country. The argument relates to tactics rather than economics. Certain objections to it may, however, be mentioned.

(a) In bargaining it is usually impossible for the country to negotiate with the rest of the world as a whole. The injury which a country suffers—in the absence of special circumstances—from a given import duty of her own is equal to that which she suffers from a like duty in all other countries and is therefore much greater than that which she suffers from a like import duty in one other particular country.[1] Therefore, if she imposes this injury on herself, she runs the risk of a great evil, if the negotiation fails, in order to gain a comparatively slight good, if the negotiation succeeds.

But, unless the foreign tariff which she seeks to get reduced has merely been imposed as a piece of bluff in answer to or to anticipate her own bluff (in which case the whole procedure is a mere waste of time), the negotiation is not likely to succeed. For the other country either does reap, owing to special circumstances, or supposes herself to reap some real advantage from the duty, or the duty is buttressed by vested interests. The real benefit which the home country has to offer the foreign country

---

[1] Import duties are said to be " like " when they are of the same *ad valorem* rate and affect imports of roughly the same value.

by reducing her duty must be small compared with this real or imaginary benefit which the foreign country gains by hers. Or, in other words, the *change* in the foreign country's economic conditions which we can offer to bring about by reducing our duty is small compared with the change which she will bring upon herself by reducing a like duty of her own. Such negotiations are therefore doomed to failure.

Of course, if the negotiating countries are prepared to embark on an elaborate system of tariff discrimination against each other, each country having a different tariff against every other, then they could offer each other in bargaining a real *quid pro quo*. But no country would embark on a career of complicated tariff discrimination, which really desired to secure a reduction of foreign tariffs against her goods. For by doing so she would render herself ineligible for Most Favoured Nation treatment in any form by foreign countries; yet this treatment is the most potent weapon by which countries do in fact secure for themselves favourable conditions in foreign countries; for by it they get the advantage not only of those reductions gained by their own bargaining, but of the sum of all reductions gained by the bargaining of all other countries.[1]

(*b*) Experience has shown that the imposition of *tarifs de combat* has in fact resulted in a raising and not a lowering of tariff levels all round.

(*c*) The method of *tarif de combat* is diametrically

---

[1] The view which has recently gained ground that it is desirable to modify the Most Favoured Nation clause, so as to allow some discrimination, follows logically from the rising hope that it may be possible to secure tariff reduction by sectional agreements.

opposed to those methods which the League of Nations is seeking to pursue. It is analogous to the method of securing general disarmament by embarking on large armament programmes. Of the wisdom and expediency of adopting such a method readers must judge for themselves.

It would probably not secure much favour in the popular judgment were it not confused with a quite different and wholly fallacious notion that the benefits which accrue to a country from not having tariffs are in some way destroyed by the existence of tariffs elsewhere. In this matter the analogy of armament breaks down. There is much to be said for being well armed just because the rest of the world is armed. The existence of foreign tariffs, while in itself an admitted evil for the home country, if imposed on goods which she does or would otherwise export, does not prevent her maintenance of free imports from being beneficial. The reader is referred to the reasoning of pages 47–49. The existence of tariffs elsewhere may reduce the total gain from foreign trade which it is open to the country to secure. Whether there are tariffs elsewhere or not, she can only realize the total gain which *is* open to her by not having tariffs herself.[1]

§ 3. *Tariffs and the best Distribution of Productive Resources.* For the rest, it may be well to divide the considerations regarding tariffs into two parts. (i) Are tariffs

[1] To quote an admirable analogy given in Beveridge, *Tariffs, The Case Examined*—if foreign countries allowed their harbours to get silted up, thus imposing a severe obstruction to the import of goods, the effect would be injurious to Great Britain. But it would not be a valid argument for allowing her own harbours to get so silted up as to impede the trade which was still possible.

likely to bring about a better distribution among occupations of a given flow of productive resources ? (ii) Are tariffs likely to increase the employment of productive resources ? This division corresponds with the general division of the treatment of the subject of international trade in this volume.

The broad answer to the first question has already been given in Chapters II and III. Two conditions were shown to be requisite for the best distribution of productive resources among occupations, namely (a) that the ratios of the prices at which home-produced goods are offered should be equal to the ratios at which they are available in the world market, and (b) the prices at which home-produced goods are offered should be proportional to their costs of production.

(a) The first condition is completely secured by free trade ; for under free trade prices at home and abroad tend not to differ by more than the cost of transport and marketing between the home and foreign centres ; the prices of home-produced goods tend to be absolutely equal to those of foreign-produced goods on the frontier of competition whether that frontier lie in the home market or in foreign markets or partly in both.

One limitation to this general doctrine must, however, be recognized. By imposing tariffs on imports, members of a community form themselves into a kind of consumers' monopoly and stint themselves in the purchase of this class of goods. Is it possible that by foregoing some advantageous purchases, they can get a sufficient reduction of the foreign offer price to compensate them for the loss ? This is another way of putting the question—can the foreigner be made to bear a portion of the tax, and will there be a net gain to the community if he does ?

If a tax is suddenly imposed, foreigners may have stocks of goods intended for the protected market which they are willing to dispose of at an exceptionally low price. They may have plant designed for the manufacture of such goods which they will be willing to work at an exceptionally low profit rather than put it out of commission. To estimate the probable effect of the tariff *in the long run*, it is necessary to refer to the underlying forces governing the comparative movement of prices at home and abroad, when channels of trade are opened or closed. These were examined at some length in Chapter II. By far the most important governing condition is the size of the home country's market compared with that of the world market for the commodities in question. Secondly, we have to take into account the elasticities of demand and supply at home and abroad. On the assumption of equal elasticities, the ratio of the fall in the foreign price of goods which the home country imports (measured in terms of goods which she exports) to the rise in the home price (so computed) will be equal to the ratio of the size of the home market to the size of the world market. If the home market is one-tenth of the world market, home prices may be expected to rise by $\frac{10}{11}$ths of the tariff and foreign prices to fall by $\frac{1}{11}$th. The greater the elasticity of home demand and supply compared with foreign demand and supply, the less the home rise and the greater the foreign fall in price.

In the new equilibrium the price of home goods exceeds that of the foreign goods by the amount of the tariff (unless the tariff is absolutely prohibitive), whereas in the old equilibrium the home price was equal to the foreign price. (Any difference due to cost of transport will be the same in both situations and may be neglected in computing the incidence of the change.) This change is made up of a home rise of $\frac{10}{11}$ths of the tax and a foreign fall of $\frac{1}{11}$th. Consequently the foreign goods which continue to come in after the tariff has been imposed will be available at a price, which will be less than the old price by an amount equal to $\frac{1}{11}$th of the tariff. The foreigner is in fact bearing $\frac{1}{11}$th of the tax. The goods will not indeed be cheaper to the consumer, since before they reach him they have to pay the duty. But the duty accrues to government which may remit taxation in other directions. To the community there is a gain of $\frac{1}{11}$th of the tariff on the foreign taxed goods which continue to come in.

On the other hand the home production of these goods will be stimulated by a rise of price equal to $\frac{10}{11}$ths of the tariff. Goods produced under the stimulus of the tariff will cost more than the goods of that class formerly produced at home by an amount varying between 0 and $\frac{10}{11}$ths of the tariff. For simplicity we may suppose the extra cost of producing these goods to be on average $\frac{5}{11}$ths of the tariff.[1] Put otherwise, the cost at which the protected goods are produced at home will exceed the cost of producing the goods previously exported in exchange for them by $\frac{5}{11}$ths of the tariff. Thus there is a gain of $\frac{1}{11}$th of the tariff on the foreign goods still imported and a loss of $\frac{5}{11}$ths of the tariff on the goods produced under the stimulus of protection. There is consequently a net gain if the goods still imported exceed five times the quantity of extra goods produced under the influence of protection. Thus a low tariff imposed by a country of considerable importance in the world economy may be

[1] Cf. computations in ch. II, pp. 23–27.

made to yield a modicum of gain.[1] The smaller the
country the lower the tariff would have to be to satisfy
this condition.[2]

It has been taken for granted that after the tariff is
imposed home prices (i.e. the prices of import goods in
terms of export goods) will exceed world prices by the
amount of the tariff. This must be so unless the tariff is
absolutely prohibitive. If it is prohibitive, home prices
and costs may not rise by the full amount of the tariff
and the loss will not be so great. On the other hand,
since no foreign goods are then bought, there will be no
gain whatever to set off against the loss.[3]

It should be noted that any gain that accrues to a
tariff-imposing country under this head is made at the
expense of the world as a whole. If the tariff provokes
retaliation there will be a net loss both to the whole and
all the parts.

(b) If prices fail to correspond to costs (second condition for best distribution of productive resources), factors
in certain occupations must be getting higher rewards
per unit of service than those in others. Adam Smith
held that the natural forces of competition would secure

---

[1] The foregoing argument neglects the loss of " Consumer's
surplus " due to the tariff ; when this is taken into account, it
appears that the scope for gainful tariff-making is still further
restricted.

[2] E.g., if the world market was 100 times as great as that
of the particular country, the tariff must on the simplest assumption be so low that the quantity of taxed foreign goods still
imported is 50 times as great as the quantity of goods produced
under the stimulus of protection.

[3] The view, often expressed, that an import duty may give
protection without raising the price of the protected commodity
at home is not deemed worthy of refutation.

equality of rewards in different occupations and so bring about the best distribution of the factors among them. It may be held, however, that this distribution will not always occur.

In particular it was argued by the German writer, List,[1] that an agrarian country would not spontaneously turn its resources towards industrialization with sufficient rapidity, owing to inertia and lack of knowledge. He recommended the protection of manufacturing industry by tariffs during the transitional phase of growth. List's doctrine became known as the Infant Industry Argument and was incorporated by J. S. Mill in his *Principles of Political Economy*. List held that the tariffs should be removed when the country attained a certain measure of manufacturing strength. His argument would not apply to the protection of a particular industry, which happened to be undeveloped ; when industrial knowledge and intelligence has reached a certain degree of cultivation, it may be expected to discover which infants are worth rearing.

The scene has really shifted since List's day. He lived in the early days of the expansion of what may roughly be classed as the B industries. It is probable that with the growing wealth of the world the day has come, at least in the advanced countries, for a relative expansion of the C industries. These cannot be assisted by protection.

More generally it might be argued, as explained in Chapter III of this volume, that there is always a lag in the shift of productive resources from declining to rising occupations and that some external stimulus would be beneficial to hasten the transfer. Such considerations must be attended with grave doubt and uncertainty.

[1] Germs of his doctrine are to be found in Hamilton's *Report on Manufactures*, 1794, U.S.A.

Tariff-making bodies are fallible; the criterion offered for their guidance is vague; this theory of protection requires them to "spot the winner" which has been overlooked; they are also liable to political pressure which interested parties are not slow to exert. Only when or if tariff-making bodies had very complete knowledge of the internal conditions and costs in particular industries, and, perhaps, some measure of control over their policy, could beneficial results be hoped for along these lines.

It was also shown in Chapter III that insufficient productive resources are employed in industries in which a monopolistic element is present and, more broadly, in those the market for whose goods is incompletely organized.[1] The more complete the monopoly, the more it should, in the community's interest, be whipped into producing more. Protection is a gentle form of castigation.

If the industry which is deemed to require stimulation neither has nor entertains hope of having an export business, a tariff on competitive imports is a certain and effective method of giving it the stimulus. On the other hand the claim of such an industry to merit stimulation is likely to be open to doubt.

Repercussions of the tariff must not be neglected. It is not impossible that some industries which ought to be stimulated are export industries. These, of course, cannot be stimulated by protection. But the protection given to others may actually impede them, if any of the protected goods enter into their cost of production. That protection will impede certain other industries is admitted in the type of protectionist case that we are examining. But it

[1] Cf. ch. III pp. 54–58.

should not be forgotten that these others may include those which have as good a case for assistance as those protected.

Since in this section we are considering the tariff not as an engine for reducing the real reward to factors, but for redistributing productive resources among their occupations, we may assume that rewards to factors will be raised by a sufficient amount to cover the higher prices of protected goods. The rise in money rewards to factors will further hamper the export industries, some of which may deserve the opposite fate.

There is also the case in which identical commodities are both imported and exported. This may be due to the distance of frontiers and the transporting costs involved (e.g. coal in Germany) or to special conditions of goodwill. In this case protection may intensify competition in the foreign markets.

§ 4. *Tariffs and the Full Utilization of Productive Resources.* Stress has recently been laid on the claim that protection has power to increase the volume of employment in the country.

A sharp distinction must be drawn according as whether, when a tariff is introduced, money rewards to factors in the country are raised by enough to cover the higher prices of protected articles and maintain the old standard of living, or not.

If rewards are raised, the tariff is not likely, except in special circumstances, to increase the volume of employment. If, on the other hand, rewards are not raised and the tariff is used as an engine for the illicit reduction of rewards to factors, its power to give increased employment need not be challenged. The questions

standard of living is consequently allowed to drop, a tariff may have a stimulating effect on employment. Since there is no change in the relation of efficiency rewards to world prices, A and B output for world markets may go on much as before. This output will indeed be impeded if the raw materials rise in price owing to the tariff. Let us suppose that a full drawback on all taxed goods used in a productive process is allowed. This supposition goes far beyond what tariff makers are usually prepared to grant, even in theory, to say nothing of practice, by way of drawbacks. They usually think of drawbacks as confined to taxed goods embodied in A and B exports. In principle, producers making A and B goods of the export class for the home market or making A and B goods subject to foreign competition in the home market have an equal claim to them.

A and B output for world markets proceeds then as before. But the tariff raises the price of certain A and B goods in the home market, and this enlarges the possibility of A and B output for that market. Consequently A and B output as a whole and the general level of employment and income in the country rises. An increase of employment has been secured at the price of a fall in the rates of reward of those in employment.

Free-trade controversialists have sometimes gone too far in denying the possibility that tariffs might give a stimulus to employment. Most tariff discussion represents a reversion to such a low type of economic thinking, that the party of truth may well be excused for an occasional exaggeration. If, it is claimed, tariffs tend to keep imports away, exports must fall off by an equal amount, and the gain of employment in the protected trades will be offset by a loss of employment in the export trades. This argument is only sound, on the assumption that the tariff does reduce the volume of imports. But it may not do so; and indeed if it does not entail directly or indirectly a rise of costs to the export industries, it is not likely to do so. Exports will be maintained and, since exports and imports balance, so also will imports. If exports are maintained, imports must be maintained also, unless the tariff leads to an exodus of capital from the country.

Imports will certainly suffer a curtailment in the first instance. The active balance so generated, it is argued, will be covered by an inflow of money, and this will tend through the action of the banking system to raise rewards to factors, and so costs of production, and so curtail exports. If this effect ensues, *cadit quæstio*. Once it is allowed that rewards to factors are raised, it cannot be claimed that protection produces a net rise in employment. But it has already been argued in another connection that an active or passive balance does not necessarily have the effect of changing the level of rewards to factors. As the price level rises, trade unions and other bodies concerned may press for and achieve rises in rewards, and the stimulating effect of the tariff may be countered. But it is a mistake to envisage such rises as necessary and automatic effects of the imposition of a tariff. It remains to consider how equilibrium is restored if such rises do not occur.

Here is the dilemma. Tariffs undoubtedly tend to keep out imports. Yet, if there is no force operating to check exports, imports will as surely be maintained. The solution is that tariffs will not in the long run reduce the volume of imports. They will merely reduce the proportion of his income that a representative man spends on imports. If tariffs are imposed in a time of unemployment, new employment will become available in the protected trades, there will be consequential new employment in the C industries, and the total volume of income will continue to rise, until the amount spent on imports reaches its old level. In the new state of affairs a smaller proportion, but the same amount, of income will be spent on imports.

The reader must not fly to the conclusion that we have here a good argument for the imposition of tariffs in a time of unemployment. For there are other and better methods of achieving the same result.

The great defect of the tariff method is that, instead of distributing the new employment among industries in the proportions which will make that employment yield the largest income, it concentrates it unduly in particular industries. Another defect is that it is a cure for depression which cannot be repeated. Once a country has by tariffs sacrificed all the gain to be derived from foreign trade, it can go no further. And when depression and unemployment continue to recur, as usual, the authorities will have to look round for new recipes. How much better had they adopted those other recipes in the first instance, instead of first imposing on their subjects the great and permanent loss connected with the sacrifice of all the benefits of foreign trade! It should be noted that it is usually considered improper to give as a cure for a temporary malady a medicine which inflicts permanent injury on the constitution. Tariff-doctors should remember that maxim.

But we have forgotten the doctors' stock reply. The tariffs can presently be removed!

o

What are the other recipes ? They all involve, directly or indirectly, some real reduction in the unadjustable rewards to factors. (In a completely collectivist state, where there are no profits, they would involve a reduction in *all* rewards.) In many cases it may be argued that it is better to sacrifice the full utilization of productive resources for the sake of maintaining rewards as they are, and to rely on rising productivity to make fuller utilization possible at the existing level of rewards in the course of time.

A fall of rewards may be secured by an outright reduction of money rewards. It cannot be denied that an *all-round* reduction of this kind is not easy to secure in an individualist economy, involves serious questions of equity as between unadjustable rewards and profits, and should in fairness be accompanied by a legal revision of all contracts. The other recipe has already been discussed in the two preceding chapters.

The serious and apparently insuperable difficulty of getting an equitable all-round reduction in money rewards throughout the community on the one hand, and our gold fetters on the other, suggested in the years 1930–31 that tariffs might after all be worth adopting as a last desperate expedient to stimulate employment in an unparalleled depression. With the fall of the gold standard in September 1931, the arguments in favour of tariffs as instruments for relieving unemployment disappeared into thin air. The authorities had *carte blanche*. They could fix the foreign exchange at whatever rate would put the home level of rewards into a reasonable relation to world prices.

Monetary policy is the appropriate instrument for securing full utilization of productive resources. It lacks the two major defects of tariff policy. It does not concentrate employment in unsuitable occupations, and its efficacy is not exhausted by use.

It might be objected that it is dangerous to put into the hands of possibly unsympathetic authorities the power of reducing real rewards to factors by " monkeying with the currency." This objection may be met. At a time when there is every prospect of real productivity continuing to rise, the rule could be laid down that when operating their policy the authorities are never to reduce real rewards.[1] It will be sufficient that they should be authorized to prevent such fortuitous increases, as exceed the limits which they regard as allowable. The details of this have already been discussed. One proviso, however, is necessary. If the authorities are to work their system properly, the starting point must be a time of full employment. To secure such a starting point in the first instance some initial reduction of real rewards may be unavoidable. Such a reduction should be definitely recognized as an extraordinary expedient, necessary to usher in a new regime. In the absence of a gold standard there can be no case for reducing real rewards by the tariff method.

§ 5. *Conclusions.* To sum up, the best distribution of productive resources and the best utilization of the opportunities offered by foreign trade are secured if (i) home offer prices are equated to foreign offer prices at the margin of competition, whether at home or abroad, and (ii) home offer prices are proportional to the costs of production at home. The first of these conditions is

---

[1] Some modification to this rule should perhaps be allowed in a period of world slump, cf. ch. VII, sec. 2, sub-sec. vii.

secured by free trade. But it is necessary to add the limiting clause that a low tariff in a large and important country may, by turning the ratio of international exchange in the country's favour, bring in a gain which more than offsets the loss due to the maldistribution of her resources which it causes. A tariff to secure this object is in truth predatory, since the loss due to the maldistribution of productive resources is absolute, while the national gain due to the turn in the terms of trade is offset by foreign loss.

Free trade encourages but does not secure the proportionality of home offer prices to costs of production. The protection of trades, rewards in which are at a relatively high level, might be favoured as a means of inducing them to produce more. The fair working of such a system would, however, be attended with great difficulties. Objections might also be raised to it on the score of equity.

Tariffs may be favoured as a method of increasing the volume of employment in the country. They are not likely to do this if money rewards to factors are raised sufficiently to cover the higher cost of living. But, if real rewards are allowed to fall, the flow of employment may be increased. This effect could, however, be more easily and more equitably effected by a reduction in the par of exchange. This expedient is free from the two major defects of the tariff method : it does not divert the productive resources of the country into less profitable channels, and it does not exhaust its own efficacy by use.

APPENDIX

THE principles on which the calculations in Chapter II are based may be explained as follows :

When the output of one commodity, B, is increased in England by an amount Q, it is assumed that the output of A is reduced in England by an amount equal to $\frac{Q}{r}$, where r is the rate at which B is exchanged for A in the new state of affairs. r is the cost of producing A divided by the cost of producing B and is referred to throughout Chapter II as " the ratio."

If the cost gradient of A is equal to that of B (simplest assumption), and if an increase in the output of B by Q leads to a rise in the cost of B by an amount q, when the output of A is decreased by $\frac{Q}{r}$ its cost falls by $\frac{q}{r}$

If the initial ratio of costs in England is represented by 1 : 1 (=1), the new relation of costs is expressed by the following equation :

$$\frac{1-\dfrac{q}{r}}{1+q}=r\dots\dots\dots\dots\dots(1)$$

From this it follows that

$$q=\frac{(r)\,(1-r)}{r^2+1}$$

If the cost gradients of sources in England are equal to those abroad, and a given amount of output is transferred from England to the outer world, a change in the English cost of a given amount is accompanied by a change in the foreign cost of that amount multiplied by n, where n is a fraction showing the ratio of England's initial output to the initial foreign output (=the number of sources in England divided by the number abroad).

If the initial ratio of the foreign cost of A to that of B is $1 : p$, the relation of foreign costs which accompanies the state of affairs represented in (1) above is expressed by the following equation :

$$\frac{1+n\dfrac{q}{r}}{p-nq}=r \; (*)\dots\dots\dots\dots(2)$$

From this it follows that

$$q=\frac{(r)\,(pr-1)}{n(r^2+1)}$$

From equations (1) and (2) it may be deduced that

$$r=\frac{1+n}{p+n}\dots\dots\dots\dots\dots(3)$$

Example : Suppose trade is opened when costs at home are $1 : 1$ and costs abroad $1 : 2$ and $n=\frac{1}{10}$ (cf. Table X, p. 29).

$$r=\frac{1+\frac{1}{10}}{2+\frac{1}{10}}=\frac{11}{21}=1 : 1\frac{10}{11}$$

$$\text{and by (1), } q=\frac{\left(\frac{11}{21}\times\frac{10}{21}\right)}{\left(\frac{11}{21}\right)^2+1}$$

$$=\frac{110}{562}=\cdot196\dots\dots$$

* If cost elasticity instead of cost gradient were used, the left-hand denominator would run $p(1-nq)$.

Consequently costs relations will be as follows :

	In England.	Abroad.
A	$\{1-(\cdot196.)(\frac{21}{11})\}x$	$\{1+(\cdot196..)(\frac{1}{10})(\frac{21}{11})\}y$
B	$\{1+(\cdot196...)\}x$	$\{2-(\cdot196...)(\frac{1}{10})\}y$

i.e.

	In England.	Abroad.
A	$\cdot625...x$	$1\cdot037..y$
B	$1\cdot196...x$	$1\cdot980..y$

If cost gradients in England are not equal to those abroad, let g stand for the average English gradient divided by the average foreign gradient over the relevant range.* Then a foreign change in costs of nq would be accompanied by an English change of gq, etc. The cost relations would be represented by the equations :

$$\frac{1-g\frac{q}{r}}{1+gq} = \frac{1+n\frac{q}{r}}{p-nq} = r$$

It follows that

$$r = \frac{g+n}{gp+n}$$

Example : if $p=5$, $n=\frac{1}{10}$ and $g=2$ (cf. Table XII, p. 32)

$$r = \frac{2+\frac{1}{10}}{10+\frac{1}{10}} = \frac{21}{101} = 1 : 4\frac{17}{21}$$

$$q = \frac{(r)(1-r)}{g(r^2+1)}$$

$$= \frac{(\frac{21}{101})(\frac{80}{101})}{2(\frac{21}{101})^2+1} = \frac{1680}{21284} = \cdot079...$$

* Demand considerations may be neglected by supposing that each demand gradient is proportional to its appropriate cost gradient

Cost relations will be as follows :

	In England.	Abroad.
A	$\left\{ 1-(\cdot079..)\,(2)\,(\frac{1}{2}\,\frac{0}{0}\,\frac{1}{1}) \right\}x$	$\left\{ 1+(\cdot079..)\,(\frac{1}{10})\,(\frac{1}{2}\,\frac{0}{0}\,\frac{1}{1}) \right\}y$
B	$\left\{ 1+(\cdot079..)\,(2) \right\}x$	$\left\{ 5-(\cdot079..)\,(\frac{1}{10}) \right\}y$

i.e.

	In England.	Abroad.
A	$\cdot24...x$	$1\cdot038..y$
B	$1\cdot158..x$	$4\cdot992..y$

QUESTIONS ON THE APPENDIX

[The demand gradient is assumed to be proportional to the cost gradient in each case.]

1. If the foreign output is initially twenty times the size of the home output, the pre-trade home cost ratio 1 : 1 and the pre-trade foreign cost ratio 1 : 4, and the cost gradients of sources equal at home and abroad, what will the new equilibrium ratio be ?

2. If the foreign output is initially four times the size of the home output, the pre-trade ratio of the cost of producing A to that of producing B at home 1 : 1 and the corresponding pre-trade foreign ratio 1 : 3, and the cost gradients of sources equal at home and abroad, what will the home and foreign costs of A and B be in the new equilibrium position ? (Assume that the pre-trade costs are expressed as x and x at home and y and $3y$, abroad.)

Estimate the cost of procuring A by importation as a fraction of the cost of making it at home before the opening of trade, assuming that the cost gradients are straight lines.

3. In which circumstances would a country gain more from the opening of foreign trade in two commodities, whose home cost ratio was initially 1 : 1 and whose foreign cost ratio was initially 1 : 3, (i) if foreign output was initially twenty times the size of home output and home cost gradients half as steep

as foreign cost gradients on the average over the relevant range, or (ii) if foreign output was initially fifteen times the size of home outputs and cost gradients at home and abroad both equal to the foreign cost gradients supposed in the first alternative ?

ANSWERS

1. $1 : 3\frac{6}{7}$

2.   At Home.   Abroad.

Cost of A $\frac{45}{97}x$ $1\frac{13}{97}y$
Cost of B $1\frac{20}{97}x$ $2\frac{92}{97}y$

(Ratio $1 : 2\frac{3}{5}$.)

$\frac{535}{923}$.

3. The former.   (The ratio is more favour in (ii) by $\frac{5}{113}$ths. But the amount of the foreign commodity purchased on the first alternative is about one and a half times as much as on the second.)

INDEX

A commodities :
  definition of, 59–60
  price level of, 62–65
Accepting houses, 91–92
Active balance, definition of,
  83
Agriculture, 52–53.

B commodities :
  definition of, 60–61
  price level of, 65–67
  peculiarities of, 67, 76, 143,
    192
Bank of England, 89, 100,
  117–118
Beveridge, Sir W., 187
Bills of exchange, 90–93
Bimetallism, 182

C commodities :
  definition of, 61–62
  price level of, 67–71
Cassel, G., 141
Central Bank, 9, 85–89, 99–
  102, 116–117, 121, 122,
  127–129, 138–141, 178–
  179
Comparative costs, law of, 14–
  20
Cost elasticity, 25, 204

Cost gradient, 24, 25, 31–35,
  203–206
  ratio, 19, 203
Costs :
  constant, 37–39
  decreasing, 37–39, 56, 67,
    168
  increasing, 21, 25
  of growth, 37
  of salesmanship, 20, 65–66
  of transport, 20, 64
Cycle. *See* Trade cycle.

Debasement of coinage, 182
Decreasing costs. *See* Costs
Deflation, 116–118, 121, 127–
  136, 178
Demand, 35–37, 205
Diminishing Returns, 146
Discount, rate of, 101–102,
  116–118
  See also Interest, rate of
Drawbacks, 197
Dumping, 48, 66

Einzig, P., 89
Exploitation, 74
Export Board, 44

Factors of production. *See*
  Rewards

Fisher, Professor Irving, 165
Forward Exchange, 93–96
Free Trade, 43–44, 58, 188

Gold exchange standard, 88–90
Gold points, 85–90
Government borrowing, 157–158, 180

h, definition of, 106
  references to, 112–115, 130, 135, 138, 144–145, 175
Hamilton, A., 192
Henderson, H. D., 29
Hungarian currency, 89

Import Board, 44
—— quotas, 134–135
Indemnity payment, 119–121
Index numbers, 166–172
Indian currency, 90
Industries, sheltered and unsheltered, 47, 69
Infant industry argument, 50, 192
Inflation, 78, 167, 170
Interest, rate of, 127, 131, 156
  See also Discount, rate of
International bank, 178
—— exchange, ratio of, 33
Invisible items, 82

Keynes, J. M., 63, 89, 122

Labour, sweated, 49
Laissez-faire, 140, 151
League of Nations, 187
List, F., 192
Loveday, A., 52

Market, unorganised, 57, 60–61, 65, 148, 168
Mill, J. S., 34, 192
Mint, English, 89
Monopoly, 54–58, 66, 168, 193
Most Favoured Nation clause, 186
Mun, T., 183

Overpopulation, 146
Overproduction, 168

Par of exchange, 85–90
Productive resources :
  best distribution of, 10–58, 187–194
  full utilization of, 75–80, 104–181, 194–202
Profit, 46, 49–54, 74–78, 105–106, 144
Protection, 49, 50
  See also Tariffs
Purchasing Power Parity theory, 70–71

Quantity theory of money, 63
Quotas. See Import

Ratio. See Cost ratio
—— of international exchange, 33
Raw materials, 53–54
Reflation, 154–157
Rent, 27
Reichsbank, 88
Rentiers, 144
Rewards to factors of production, 7, 45–47, 71–80, 104–113, 124–125, 141, 143–145, 194–202

Ricardo, D., 20, 170, 184

Robinson, E. A. G., 37

Royal Institute of International Affairs, 164

Safeguarding, British policy of, 50

Sinking Fund, 158

Smith, Adam, 11, 184, 185, 191

Sterling exchange standard, 89–90

Tariffs, 30, 34, 64–65, 120, 134, 176, 182–202

Tarifs de combat, 185–187

Telegraphic transfer, 91

Trade Cycle, 159–162

Transport costs. *See* Costs

Undervaluation of currency, 103

Unemployment, 51–52, 76–77, 109–115, 119–121, 126–128, 194–202

United States Department of Commerce, 82

Wages, 7, 51–54, 71–80